BOGOTÁ

TRAVEL GUIDE

2024 EDITION

Bogotá Escapade: Immersive Experiences, Local Delights, and Hidden Treasures Await

ROXANNE AZURE

Table of Contents

Important Notice Before Reading

Embark on a literary journey with "Bogotá Escapade," where words weave a tapestry of experiences. This guide intentionally skips images and maps, inviting you to create your mental canvas. Immerse yourself in the art of storytelling, where each description sparks your imagination. Your mind is the guide, and every word paints a vivid picture of Bogotá's wonders. Welcome to a visual feast crafted by your imagination – where the absence of visuals enhances the power of the narrative. Dive into "Bogotá Escapade" and let your imagination be the ultimate navigator!

Introduction

Welcome to Bogotá, the dynamic and pulsating capital of Colombia! Nestled in the heart of the Andean region, this high-altitude metropolis at over 2,600 meters above sea level offers a captivating blend of history, culture, and modernity. As you embark on your journey through Bogotá, prepare to be enthralled by the city's rich tapestry of experiences, from the cobblestone streets of the historic La Candelaria district to the contemporary vibrancy of Zona T.

Bogotá is a city that unfolds like a story, with each neighborhood revealing a different chapter of Colombia's narrative. La Candelaria, the historical center, beckons with its colonial charm and iconic landmarks, while neighborhoods like Chapinero and Usaquén showcase the city's diversity and modern flair.

Dive into Bogotá's cultural mosaic through its world-class museums, vibrant street art, and immersive theaters. Explore the Gold Museum's treasures, wander through graffiti-covered alleys in La Candelaria, or attend a performance at Ciudad Teatro for a taste of the city's artistic richness.

Bogotá's culinary scene is a gastronomic journey waiting to be explored. From the bustling Paloquemao Market, where fresh produce and exotic flavors converge, to the upscale dining establishments in Zona G, the city offers a diverse palate that reflects Colombia's culinary diversity.

Get acquainted with Bogotá's layout, where numbered Carreras and Calles form a structured grid system. Understand the significance of each neighborhood, from the historical significance of La Candelaria to the modern allure of Zona Rosa.

As the sun sets, Bogotá transforms into a nightlife haven. Zona T pulsates with energy as bars and clubs come to life, offering a glimpse into the city's contemporary spirit. Cafes, too, provide intimate spaces for conversations and sipping Colombian coffee, fostering a unique blend of old and new.

This guide is your key to unlocking Bogotá's secrets. Whether you're a history enthusiast, a food lover, or a night owl seeking the city's vibrant pulse, our comprehensive guide will navigate you through the must-see attractions, culinary delights, and cultural wonders that make Bogotá an unforgettable destination.

Get ready to decode the essence of Bogotá – a city where history meets modernity, and every street corner tells a story. Let the adventure begin!

Chapter 1

Getting Acquainted with Bogotá

Brief History Unveiled

Bogotá, the pulsating heart of Colombia, is a city whose history is as diverse and intricate as its modern skyline. To truly understand the soul of this metropolis, one must delve into the rich tapestry of its past, shaped by indigenous cultures, Spanish colonization, independence struggles, and a continual evolution into the vibrant capital we see today.

Pre-Colonial Era:

Long before the arrival of Spanish conquistadors, the region that now encompasses Bogotá was inhabited by various indigenous groups, notably the Muisca people. These advanced societies thrived in the fertile highlands of the Andes, developing sophisticated agricultural practices and intricate systems of trade and governance. The Muisca are renowned for their goldwork, which played a significant role in their spiritual and economic life.

Spanish Conquest and Colonial Era:

In 1538, Spanish explorer Gonzalo Jiménez de Quesada arrived in the Altiplano Cundiboyacense, marking the beginning of Spanish rule in the region. The settlement of Santa Fé de Bogotá, as it was originally named, became an important administrative center in the Spanish colonial hierarchy. The city's strategic location on the trade route between Quito and Cartagena contributed to its rapid growth.

Throughout the colonial era, Bogotá served as the political and cultural hub of the Viceroyalty of New Granada, a vast administrative district within the Spanish Empire. The city's architecture reflected the prevailing Spanish colonial style, with churches, government buildings, and grand plazas shaping the urban landscape.

Independence and Republican Era:

Bogotá played a pivotal role in the fight for South American independence. The seeds of rebellion were sown in the early 19th century, and on July 20, 1810, a group of patriots in Bogotá initiated the movement for independence. This date is now celebrated as Colombia's Independence Day. The struggle for freedom continued for a decade, culminating in the Battle of Boyacá in 1819, which secured Colombia's independence from Spanish rule.

The 19th century marked the beginning of the Republic of Colombia, and Bogotá became the capital of the newly formed nation. The city underwent transformations, with urban development, cultural institutions, and educational facilities shaping its identity as a burgeoning center of political and intellectual activity.

20th Century and Beyond:

Bogotá's growth accelerated in the 20th century, as it transformed into a modern metropolis. The city expanded both geographically and demographically, attracting migrants from rural areas seeking economic opportunities. The mid-20th century saw significant urban development, including the construction of major infrastructure such as the TransMilenio system and the El Dorado International Airport.

However, Bogotá also faced challenges, including social inequalities and political unrest. The latter half of the 20th century was marked by periods of civil conflict and violence. In recent decades, the city has made strides in overcoming these challenges, with a focus on urban revitalization, cultural preservation, and social inclusivity.

Today, Bogotá stands as a testament to the resilience of its people and the convergence of diverse influences. Its historic neighborhoods, colonial architecture, and vibrant cultural scene coexist with modern skyscrapers, reflecting the city's ongoing journey through time. As Bogotá continues to evolve, it remains firmly rooted in its past, a living canvas that tells the story of Colombia's dynamic history.

Bogotá's Geographical Tapestry

Nestled in the scenic Andean highlands of Colombia, Bogotá boasts a unique geographical setting that significantly shapes its climate, landscape, and cultural identity. Let's embark on a journey through the city's geography and location, exploring the factors that contribute to its distinct character.

Altitude and Andean Splendor:

Bogotá is renowned as one of the highest capital cities in the world, situated at an elevation of approximately 2,640 meters (8,660 feet) above sea level. This lofty position places it in the expansive Andean plateau known as the Altiplano Cundiboyacense. The city's high altitude not only lends it a cool, temperate climate but also influences various aspects of life, including oxygen levels and the preparation of the region's unique crops.

Andean Climate:

Bogotá's altitude contributes to its pleasantly mild climate, with average temperatures ranging from 14°C to 20°C (57°F to 68°F) throughout the year. The absence of extreme temperature variations is a result of its proximity to the equator. However, it's essential for visitors to be prepared for cool evenings, especially given the city's mountainous surroundings.

Surrounded by Greenery:

The city is embraced by the Eastern Andes, a mountain range that adds to Bogotá's scenic beauty. Hills and lush greenery characterize the landscape, and within the city, the presence of numerous parks and green spaces provides residents and visitors with opportunities for outdoor activities and relaxation. Iconic peaks like Monserrate and Guadalupe offer panoramic views of the city and are popular destinations for both tourists and locals.

Bogotá River and Surrounding Savannas:

The Bogotá River, also known as the Funza, flows through the city, contributing to the fertile savannas that surround Bogotá. These savannas, or "sabanas," are part of the larger Altiplano Cundiboyacense and play a crucial role in the region's agriculture. The fertile soils support the cultivation of crops such as potatoes, carrots, and flowers, which are vital to the city's economy.

Urban Expansion and Neighborhood Diversity:

Bogotá's geographical layout is characterized by a combination of historical neighborhoods, modern districts, and residential areas. The historic district of La Candelaria, with its colonial architecture, contrasts with the contemporary skyline of the Chapinero district. Understanding the geography of the city is key to navigating its diverse neighborhoods and discovering the unique charm each one has to offer.

Transportation Challenges:

The city's mountainous terrain has also posed challenges for urban development and transportation. To address this, the city implemented the TransMilenio, a rapid bus transit system, to navigate the challenging topography and improve accessibility for residents and visitors alike.

Gateway to Colombia:

Bogotá's strategic location within Colombia positions it as a gateway to the rest of the country. The El Dorado International Airport, one of the busiest in South America, connects the city to domestic and international destinations, facilitating trade, tourism, and cultural exchange.

In essence, Bogotá's geography is not just a backdrop but an integral part of its identity. From the towering Andean peaks to the thriving savannas, every facet of the city's location contributes to the rich tapestry of experiences that await those who explore this high-altitude marvel in the heart of Colombia.

Navigating Local Customs and Etiquette in Bogotá

Embarking on a journey to Bogotá not only introduces you to its stunning landscapes and vibrant attractions but also immerses you in the rich tapestry of Colombian culture. Navigating local customs and etiquette is integral to fostering positive interactions, showing respect for the local way of life, and enhancing your overall travel experience. Here's a detailed guide to help you navigate the cultural nuances of Bogotá:

1. Greetings and Social Interactions:

- Warm and Friendly Greetings: Colombians are known for their warmth. Greet people with a smile, a firm handshake, and direct eye contact.
- Use of Titles: Address people with their titles, such as "Señor" for Mr., "Señora" for Mrs., and "Señorita" for Miss, to convey respect.

2. Punctuality and Time Perception:

- Flexible Time: While punctuality is appreciated, Colombian time can be more flexible. Be prepared for events and meetings to start a bit later than scheduled.
- Respecting Others' Time: Despite flexibility, respect others' time commitments and be considerate of schedules.

3. Dining Etiquette:

- Polite Table Manners: Maintain good table manners, including keeping your hands on the table and waiting for the host to start the meal.
- Acknowledging Hospitality: Express gratitude to your host for their hospitality, whether dining at a local home or a restaurant.

4. Gift-Giving Customs:

- Small Tokens of Appreciation: When invited to someone's home, consider bringing a small gift such as flowers, chocolates, or a souvenir from your home country.
- Open Gifts Privately: If you receive a gift, it's customary to open it in private to avoid putting the giver on the spot.

5. Communication Style:

- Expressive Communication: Colombians are generally expressive and passionate in their communication. Expect animated conversations with gestures and facial expressions.
- Respectful Tone: Use a respectful and polite tone, especially when engaging with elders or those in positions of authority.

6. Dress Code:

- Smart Casual: Bogotá has a varied climate, so dress in layers. In urban areas, smart casual attire is common. If attending a formal event, opt for more formal clothing.
- Modesty Consideration: When visiting religious sites or rural areas, dress modestly out of respect for local customs.

7. Religion and Traditions:

- Catholic Influence: Colombia is predominantly Catholic, and religious traditions play a significant role. Respect local customs, particularly during religious festivals and ceremonies.
- Festive Celebrations: Participate in local celebrations and festivals to gain insight into the culture's religious and traditional dimensions.

8. Language Considerations:

- Spanish Dominance: Spanish is the official language. While many Colombians in urban areas may speak some English, it's beneficial to learn basic Spanish phrases to facilitate communication.

- Cultural Appreciation: Showing an effort to speak the local language is often appreciated and fosters positive interactions.

9. Personal Space and Physical Contact:

- Friendly Gestures: Colombians are comfortable with physical contact, such as hugs and cheek kisses, among friends and family.
- Respecting Personal Space: However, it's important to be mindful of personal space, especially when interacting with strangers or in more formal settings.

10. Music and Dance:

- Rhythmic Culture: Music and dance are integral to Colombian culture. Embrace the lively rhythms of salsa, cumbia, and vallenato.
- Participation Encouraged: Don't be shy to join in the dance when invited. It's a great way to connect with locals and experience the joyous spirit of the culture.

11. Local Markets and Bargaining:

- Polite Bargaining: In markets, bargaining is common. Approach it with politeness and a smile. It's a cultural practice, but do so respectfully.
- Appreciating Local Crafts: Take the time to appreciate the craftsmanship of local artisans and show interest in the stories behind their creations.

12. Environmental Respect:

- Eco-Friendly Mindset: Colombians value their natural surroundings. Dispose of waste responsibly, and participate in eco-friendly initiatives when possible.
- Respecting Nature: When exploring natural sites, adhere to guidelines and respect the local flora and fauna.

13. Acceptance of Diversity:

- Cultural Diversity: Colombia is ethnically diverse, and each region has its own unique customs. Embrace this diversity with an open mind and a willingness to learn.
- Avoiding Stereotypes: Be mindful of avoiding stereotypes or generalizations about Colombian culture, recognizing the richness of its multifaceted identity.

14. Courtesy in Public Spaces:

- Public Behavior: Maintain a level of courtesy in public spaces. Avoid loud conversations or disruptive behavior in places like public transport or libraries.
- Queueing Etiquette: Respect queues and wait your turn, whether in shops or public transportation.

15. Safety and Caution:

- Street Smart Practices: While generally safe, exercise standard safety precautions. Be cautious with valuables in crowded places and follow local advice regarding certain neighborhoods.

Navigating local customs and etiquette in Bogotá is an opportunity to connect with the heart of Colombian culture. By embracing the local way of life with respect and openness, you'll not only enhance your travel experience but also forge meaningful connections with the people you meet along the way.

Essential Basic Phrases

As you embark on your adventure in Bogotá, Colombia, equipping yourself with basic Spanish phrases will significantly enhance your experience and foster meaningful interactions with the locals. While many Colombians in urban areas may understand and speak some English, making an effort to communicate in their native language demonstrates cultural respect and often leads to warmer connections. Here's a beginner's guide to essential Spanish phrases tailored for your Bogotá journey:

1. Greetings and Courtesies:

- Hola (OH-lah) - Hello
- Buenos días (BWAY-nos DEE-as) - Good morning
- Buenas tardes (BWAY-nas TAR-des) - Good afternoon
- Buenas noches (BWAY-nas NOH-chess) - Good evening/night
- Por favor (por fa-VOR) - Please
- Gracias (GRAH-syas) - Thank you
- De nada (de NA-da) - You're welcome

2. Introductions and Polite Phrases:

- ¿Cómo te llamas? (COH-moh te YAH-mas) - What's your name?
- Me llamo... (may YAH-mo) - My name is...
- Mucho gusto (MOO-choh GOOS-toh) - Nice to meet you
- Disculpe (DEES-kool-pe) - Excuse me
- Perdón (pair-DON) - Pardon

3. Basic Conversation:

- Sí (SEE) - Yes
- No (NOH) - No
- ¿Cómo estás? (COH-moh es-TAHS) - How are you?
- Estoy bien, gracias (es-TOY byen, GRAH-syas) - I'm fine, thank you
- ¿Qué tal? (keh TAL) - How's it going?

4. Getting Around:

- ¿Dónde está...? (DON-de es-TA) - Where is...?
- Izquierda (ees-kyer-da) - Left
- Derecha (de-RE-cha) - Right
- Baño (BAH-nyo) - Bathroom
- Parada de autobús (pa-RA-da de ow-TO-bus) - Bus stop
- Taxi (TAK-see) - Taxi

5. Eating Out:

- ¿Qué recomienda? (keh re-koh-MEEN-da) - What do you recommend?
- La cuenta, por favor (la KWEHN-ta, por fa-VOR) - The bill, please
- Agua (AH-gwa) - Water
- Café (ca-FE) - Coffee
- La carta (la CAR-ta) - The menu

6. Shopping Phrases:

- ¿Cuánto cuesta? (KWAHN-to KWE-sta) - How much does it cost?
- ¿Tiene esto en otra talla/color? (TYE-ne EH-sto en o-tra TA-ya/KO-lor) - Do you have this in another size/color?

- Quisiera comprar esto (kee-SYE-ra kom-PRAR EH-sto) - I would like to buy this
- ¿Aceptan tarjeta de crédito? (ah-SEP-tan tar-HE-ta de KRE-di-to) - Do you accept credit cards?

7. Directions and Transportation:

- ¿Cómo llego a...? (COH-mo YEH-go a) - How do I get to...?
- Estación de tren (es-ta-SYON de tren) - Train station
- Aeropuerto (ah-eh-ro-PU-er-to) - Airport
- Autobús (ow-TO-boos) - Bus
- ¿Cuánto cuesta el boleto? (KWAHN-to KWE-sta el bo-LE-to) - How much is the ticket?

8. Emergency Phrases:

- Ayuda (ah-YU-da) - Help
- Necesito un médico (ne-se-SEE-to oon ME-di-ko) - I need a doctor
- Llame a la policía (YA-meh a la po-lee-SEE-a) - Call the police
- Hospital (os-pee-TAL) - Hospital
- Fuego (FWEH-go) - Fire

9. Numbers:

- Uno (OO-no) - One
- Dos (DOHS) - Two
- Tres (TRES) - Three
- Cuatro (KWA-tro) - Four
- Cinco (SEEN-ko) - Five
- Diez (DYEHZ) - Ten

- Cien (SYEN) - Hundred

10. Expressions of Gratitude:

- Muchas gracias (MOO-chas GRAH-syas) - Many thanks
- Gracias por todo (GRAH-syas por TO-do) - Thanks for everything
- Te lo agradezco mucho (te lo a-grade-SKO MOO-cho) - I appreciate it a lot

Learning and using these basic Spanish phrases will not only make your journey through Bogotá smoother but also open doors to authentic cultural exchanges. Colombians often appreciate the effort to communicate in their language, creating a more enriching and enjoyable experience for both you and the locals.

Chapter 2

Planning Your Trip

Choosing the Best Time to Visit Bogotá

Bogotá, nestled in the Andean highlands of Colombia, experiences a mild and temperate climate throughout the year due to its proximity to the equator. However, understanding the nuances of Bogotá's seasons and local events can significantly enhance your travel experience. Let's explore the factors that can help you choose the best time to visit this dynamic city.

1. Weather Overview:

- Dry Season (December to March, July to August): These months generally bring drier and sunnier weather, making them popular for outdoor activities and city exploration.
- Rainy Season (April to June, September to November): While rainfall is more frequent during these periods, it often comes in short, intense bursts, and the city remains lush and green.

2. Temperature Considerations:

- Year-Round Mild Climate: Bogotá's high-altitude location contributes to consistent, mild temperatures. Daytime temperatures usually range from 14°C to 20°C (57°F to 68°F).
- Cooler Evenings: Regardless of the season, evenings tend to be cooler, so packing layers is advisable.

3. Special Events and Festivals:

- Bogotá Carnival (January/February): Experience the vibrant Bogotá Carnival with colorful parades, traditional dances, and cultural celebrations.
- Bogotá International Book Fair (April): Literature enthusiasts may enjoy visiting during the book fair, a cultural event that attracts authors, publishers, and readers from around the world.
- Festival Iberoamericano de Teatro (Every Two Years, March/April): The Iberoamerican Theater Festival showcases performances from international and local artists, creating a lively cultural atmosphere.

4. Avoiding Crowds:

- High Tourist Season: The dry seasons (December to March and July to August) tend to attract more tourists. If you prefer a quieter experience, consider visiting during the shoulder seasons.

5. Natural Attractions:

- Hiking and Outdoor Activities: The dry season is ideal for hiking and outdoor adventures, providing clearer views and more stable trail conditions.
- Flora and Fauna: If you're interested in the region's biodiversity, the rainy season showcases lush landscapes and blooming vegetation.

6. Budget Considerations:

- Peak vs. Off-Peak Travel: Prices for accommodations and flights may vary depending on the season. Off-peak times might offer more budget-friendly options.

7. Local Holidays and Observances:

- Semana Santa (Holy Week): Easter week is a significant holiday in Colombia, and Bogotá may experience increased local tourism during this period.
- Independence Day (July 20): Celebrate Colombia's Independence Day with patriotic events and parades.

8. Photography Opportunities:

- Lighting Conditions: Consider the lighting conditions for photography. The dry season can provide clearer skies and more favorable lighting for capturing landmarks and landscapes.

9. Flexibility in Planning:

- Unexpected Weather: While Bogotá's climate is generally predictable, it's advisable to be flexible in your plans as weather conditions can vary.

10. Personal Preferences:

- Tolerance for Rain: If you don't mind occasional rain and enjoy the lushness it brings, the rainy season might be an attractive option.
- Outdoor vs. Indoor Activities: Your preference for outdoor activities or indoor cultural experiences can influence the best time to visit.

11. Consideration for Altitude Adjustment:

- Gradual Acclimatization: Given Bogotá's high altitude, visitors may need time to acclimate. Gradual adjustment can be facilitated by staying hydrated and avoiding strenuous activities in the first few days.

In conclusion, the best time to visit Bogotá depends on your individual preferences and interests. Whether you're drawn to cultural festivals, outdoor adventures, or a quieter exploration of the city's charms, understanding the seasonal variations and local events will help you craft an itinerary that aligns with your travel goals.

Bogotá Visa and Entry Requirements

Traveling to Bogotá, the pulsating heart of Colombia, involves understanding and adhering to the country's visa and entry requirements. Colombia, known for its warm hospitality and diverse landscapes, has streamlined its entry processes in recent years. Here's a detailed guide to help you navigate the visa and entry requirements for a seamless entry into Bogotá.

1. Visa Exemption for Short Visits:

- Tourist Visa Exemption: Citizens of many countries, including the United States, Canada, most European countries, and several others, are exempt from obtaining a tourist visa for stays of up to 90 days.
- Diplomatic and Official Passport Holders: Diplomatic and official passport holders from various countries enjoy visa exemptions for specific durations.

2. Electronic Travel Authorization (ETA):

- Colombia's Electronic Visa System: Colombia has implemented an Electronic Travel Authorization (ETA) system for certain nationalities. Check if your country is eligible for ETA and complete the online application process before traveling.

3. Visitor Visa for Longer Stays:

- Longer Stays: If you plan to stay in Colombia for more than 90 days, you may need to apply for a visitor visa before your arrival.
- Application Process: The application process for a visitor visa typically involves submitting required documents, including a passport, proof of funds, and proof of accommodation, to the Colombian consulate or embassy.

4. Business and Work Visas:

- Business Travel: Travelers visiting Bogotá for business purposes may need to obtain a business visa.
- Work Opportunities: If you intend to work in Bogotá, securing a work visa is essential. This involves collaboration with a Colombian employer who sponsors your application.

5. Passport Validity:

- Six-Month Rule: Ensure that your passport is valid for at least six months beyond your planned departure date. This is a standard requirement for entry into Colombia.

6. Entry Points and Immigration Procedures:

- Bogotá Airport (El Dorado International Airport): Most international travelers arrive in Bogotá through El Dorado International Airport. Follow the immigration procedures upon arrival, which typically include passport checks and visa verification.

7. Onward or Return Ticket Requirement:

- Proof of Departure: Immigration authorities may request proof of onward or return travel, demonstrating your intention to leave Colombia within the permitted timeframe.

8. Yellow Fever Vaccination Certificate:

- Vaccination Requirement: Travelers arriving from countries with a risk of yellow fever transmission are required to present a valid yellow fever vaccination certificate.

9. Customs and Declarations:

- Customs Form: Complete the customs form provided on the airplane, declaring any items of value or specific goods you are bringing into the country.

10. Currency Declaration:

- Cash Limit: Declare any amounts exceeding $10,000 USD upon arrival. Failure to do so may result in fines or confiscation.

11. Local Contact Information:

- Accommodation Details: Be prepared to provide details of your accommodation in Bogotá, including the address and contact information.

12. Emergency Preparedness:

- Embassy or Consulate Contacts: Keep the contact information for your country's embassy or consulate in Bogotá in case of emergencies.

13. Understanding Local Laws and Customs:

- Respect Local Laws: Familiarize yourself with local laws and customs to ensure a respectful and compliant visit to Bogotá.

14. Monitoring Travel Advisories:

- Government Websites: Regularly check your government's travel advisory website for updates on entry requirements, safety considerations, and any changes to visa policies.

Understanding and complying with Bogotá's visa and entry requirements is essential for a smooth and enjoyable visit. By staying informed, preparing the necessary documentation, and following the established procedures, you'll unlock the gateway to the vibrant culture, history, and landscapes that Bogotá has to offer.

Vaccination and Health Precautions

Prioritizing your health and well-being is paramount when planning a trip to Bogotá, Colombia. Vaccinations and health precautions play a crucial role in safeguarding against potential health risks, ensuring a smooth and enjoyable travel experience. Here's a detailed guide on vaccinations and health precautions to consider before embarking on your journey to Bogotá.

1. Routine Vaccinations:

- Check-Up with Healthcare Provider: Schedule a check-up with your healthcare provider well before your trip. Ensure that routine vaccinations, such as measles, mumps, rubella (MMR), diphtheria, tetanus, and pertussis (DTaP), and influenza, are up-to-date.

2. Yellow Fever Vaccination:

- Mandatory Requirement: Yellow fever vaccination is mandatory for travelers entering Bogotá from countries with a risk of yellow fever transmission. Ensure you receive the vaccine at least ten days before your trip and carry the International Certificate of Vaccination or Prophylaxis (ICVP) as proof.

3. Typhoid and Hepatitis A Vaccinations:

- Recommended Vaccines: Consider getting vaccinations for typhoid and hepatitis A, particularly if you plan to explore local cuisine or visit areas with potential food and water contamination risks.

4. Hepatitis B and Rabies Vaccinations:

- Optional But Recommended: Hepatitis B and rabies vaccinations are optional, but they might be advisable depending on your travel activities and duration of stay. Consult with your healthcare provider to assess the necessity.

5. Malaria Prevention:

- Antimalarial Medications: While Bogotá itself is not a malaria-endemic area, if you plan to explore other regions of Colombia, especially those at lower altitudes, consult with your healthcare provider regarding antimalarial medications.

6. Zika Virus Precautions:

- Risk Assessment: Assess the risk of Zika virus transmission in the region and take appropriate precautions. Pregnant women or those planning to become pregnant may need to reconsider travel due to potential complications.

7. Altitude Considerations:

- Bogotá's Altitude: Bogotá is situated at a high altitude (2,640 meters or 8,660 feet). If you have respiratory or cardiovascular conditions, consult with your healthcare provider to assess your readiness for high-altitude travel.

8. Travel Health Insurance:

- Comprehensive Coverage: Consider obtaining travel health insurance that provides comprehensive coverage for medical emergencies, hospitalization, and evacuation if needed.

9. Water and Food Safety:

- Safe Drinking Water: Stick to bottled or treated water to avoid waterborne illnesses. Ensure that the seals on bottled water are intact before consumption.
- Food Hygiene: Opt for well-cooked and hot foods, and avoid consuming raw or undercooked seafood, eggs, and meat.

10. Mosquito Bite Prevention:

- Protective Clothing and Repellents: Use insect repellents containing DEET, wear long-sleeved clothing, and use bed nets to minimize the risk of mosquito-borne diseases.

11. Sun Protection:

- Sunscreen and Protective Gear: Bogotá's high altitude means increased sun exposure. Use sunscreen with a high

SPF, wear sunglasses, and consider a hat to protect against UV rays.

12. Healthcare Facilities in Bogotá:

- Quality Healthcare: Bogotá has reputable healthcare facilities and medical professionals. Familiarize yourself with the locations of hospitals and clinics in case of emergencies.

13. Personal Medications:

- Carry Prescriptions: If you require prescription medications, ensure you have an adequate supply for the duration of your stay and carry prescriptions in case you need a refill.

14. COVID-19 Considerations:

- Current Guidelines: Stay informed about the latest COVID-19 guidelines and requirements for travel. This may include testing and quarantine protocols.

15. Emergency Contacts:

- Embassy and Consulate Information: Keep the contact information for your country's embassy or consulate in Bogotá in case of emergencies.

16. Local Health Precautions:

- Respect COVID-19 Measures: Abide by local health measures and guidelines in response to the COVID-19 pandemic. This may include mask-wearing, social distancing, and hand hygiene.

17. Post-Trip Health Assessment:

- Follow-Up Check-Up: Upon returning home, consider scheduling a follow-up check-up with your healthcare provider, especially if you experienced any health concerns during your trip.

By taking proactive steps, staying informed, and consulting with healthcare professionals, you can minimize health risks and ensure a safe and enjoyable journey to Bogotá. Prioritize your well-being, and you'll be better equipped to savor the vibrant culture, history, and landscapes that this Colombian capital has to offer.

Budgeting and Money Matters in Bogotá

Planning a trip to Bogotá involves careful budgeting and managing your money wisely to ensure a smooth and enjoyable experience. Here's an in-depth guide on budgeting and money matters to help you make the most of your stay in Colombia's capital:

1. Establish a Realistic Budget:

- Accommodation: Research and choose accommodation options that fit your budget. Bogotá offers a range of choices, from budget-friendly hostels to luxurious hotels.
- Meals: Plan your daily meals, considering the cost of dining out versus preparing your own. Exploring local markets for fresh produce can be a cost-effective way to experience Colombian cuisine.
- Transportation: Factor in transportation costs, including airport transfers, local transportation, and any planned excursions.

2. Currency Exchange and Payment Methods:

- Check Exchange Rates: Before your trip, monitor exchange rates and choose the most favorable time to convert your currency to Colombian Pesos (COP).
- Use ATMs: Withdraw cash from ATMs for daily expenses. ATMs in Bogotá are widely available and offer competitive exchange rates. Notify your bank before traveling to avoid any issues with international transactions.
- Credit Cards: While credit cards are accepted in many establishments, it's wise to have some cash for places that may not accept cards. Inform your credit card company about your travel plans to prevent any disruptions.

3. Daily Expense Breakdown:

- Meals: Consider the average cost of meals in Bogotá. Street food and local eateries can be more budget-friendly than upscale restaurants.
- Transportation: Budget for local transportation, including buses, taxis, or rideshare services. Additionally, allocate funds for any planned day trips or excursions.
- Attractions and Activities: Research the entrance fees and costs associated with attractions and activities you plan to visit. Some museums and landmarks may offer discounts on certain days.

4. Bargaining and Negotiating Prices:

- Local Markets: If you're shopping at local markets, bargaining is a common practice. Politely negotiate prices, but remember to be respectful of the local culture.
- Transportation: When taking taxis, negotiate the fare before starting the journey or ensure that the meter is used. Rideshare services like Uber are also available in Bogotá.

5. Tipping Etiquette:

- Restaurants: Check if a service charge is included in your restaurant bill. If not, tipping around 5-10% is customary for good service.
- Taxis: While not mandatory, rounding up the fare or adding a small tip to taxi drivers is appreciated.

6. Safety Measures:

- ATM Usage: Exercise caution when using ATMs. Choose well-lit and busy locations, and be aware of your surroundings.
- Carry a Mix of Payment Methods: Have a mix of cash and cards, and store them securely. Consider using a money belt or concealed pouch for added security.

7. Emergency Financial Contact Information:

- Lost or Stolen Cards: Have contact information for your bank readily available in case your credit or debit card is lost or stolen.
- Emergency Assistance: Know the contact information for your country's embassy or consulate in Bogotá for financial emergencies.

8. Utilize Budgeting Apps:

- Expense Tracking: Consider using budgeting apps to track your expenses in real-time. This can help you stay within your budget and make informed spending decisions.

9. Plan for Contingencies:

- Emergency Fund: Set aside a small emergency fund for unexpected expenses or situations. This can provide peace of mind and ensure you're prepared for any unforeseen circumstances.

By carefully planning and managing your budget, you can make the most of your time in Bogotá, experiencing the city's culture, cuisine, and attractions without financial stress. Flexibility is key, so allow room for spontaneity while keeping an eye on your overall spending.

Itinerary: Duration of Stay in Bogotá

Embarking on a journey to Bogotá offers a myriad of experiences, from cultural immersions to outdoor adventures. Crafting the perfect itinerary involves balancing historical explorations, culinary delights, and moments of relaxation. Below is a comprehensive guide to help you plan the ideal duration for your stay in Colombia's vibrant capital.

1. Weekend Getaway (2-3 Days)

For a brief but immersive experience, a weekend in Bogotá provides a taste of its cultural richness.

Day 1: Arrival and Cultural Immersion

- Morning: Explore La Candelaria's historic streets, visit Plaza de Bolívar, and wander through museums like the Gold Museum.
- Afternoon: Discover street art in the colorful neighborhoods of La Candelaria or visit the Botero Museum.
- Evening: Dine in a traditional Colombian restaurant and experience the vibrant nightlife in Zona Rosa.

Day 2: Nature and Relaxation

- Morning: Head to Monserrate for panoramic views of the city and explore the surrounding gardens.
- Afternoon: Enjoy a leisurely lunch in Usaquén, known for its charming atmosphere and outdoor cafés.
- Evening: Unwind with a spa experience or attend a live music performance in one of the city's cozy venues.

Day 3: Outdoor Adventures

- Morning: Visit the Paloquemao Market to experience Bogotá's culinary scene.
- Afternoon: Explore the Salt Cathedral of Zipaquirá for a unique underground adventure.
- Evening: Reflect on your journey over a farewell dinner in one of Bogotá's acclaimed restaurants.

2. Cultural Immersion (5-7 Days)

- A longer stay allows for a deeper dive into Bogotá's cultural treasures and nearby attractions.

Days 1-3: Historical Exploration

- Explore La Candelaria's museums, churches, and colonial architecture.
- Take guided tours to learn about Bogotá's history and street art scene.

Days 4-5: Culinary Delights

- Experience Bogotá's diverse food scene with culinary tours and visits to local markets.
- Attend cooking classes to learn about traditional Colombian dishes.

Days 6-7: Day Trips and Nature

- Take a day trip to Zipaquirá for the Salt Cathedral and nearby attractions.
- Explore the lush landscapes of Chingaza National Park for a nature retreat.

3. Comprehensive Journey (10+ Days)

For a more comprehensive exploration, extending your stay allows for day trips to surrounding areas.

Days 1-5: Bogotá's Cultural Core

- Delve into La Candelaria's historical richness and explore lesser-known neighborhoods.
- Attend cultural events, theater performances, and local festivals.

Days 6-8: Culinary and Outdoor Adventures

- Immerse yourself in Bogotá's culinary scene with extended cooking classes.
- Embark on day trips to nearby coffee plantations and explore traditional markets.

Days 9-12: Surrounding Regions

- Explore the coffee region, visiting towns like Salento and hiking in Cocora Valley.
- Head to Villa de Leyva for its charming cobblestone streets and historical significance.

Practical Tips:

- Weather Considerations: Bogotá has a moderate climate, but it's essential to check the weather for day trips or outdoor activities.

- Transportation: Plan your itinerary considering traffic and transportation options. Public transport, taxis, and ride-sharing apps are readily available.
- Local Events: Check for local events, festivals, and exhibitions happening during your stay to enhance your cultural experience.

Bogotá's allure lies in its diverse offerings, and tailoring your itinerary to your interests ensures a memorable and enriching stay in this vibrant Colombian capital. Whether you're a weekend explorer or an extended traveler, Bogotá welcomes you with open arms and a wealth of experiences to discover.

Chapter 3

Transportation Options

Getting to Bogotá

Bogotá, the vibrant capital of Colombia, is a major hub with various transportation options catering to both domestic and international travelers. Whether you're arriving by air, land, or sea, Bogotá offers convenient and diverse ways to reach the city. Here's a detailed exploration of transportation options to help you plan your journey to this South American metropolis:

1. Air Travel: El Dorado International Airport:

Overview:

- Location: El Dorado International Airport (BOG) is located about 15 kilometers west of Bogotá's city center.
- Facilities: El Dorado is one of the busiest airports in Latin America, equipped with modern facilities, lounges, shops, and services.
- Airlines: Numerous international airlines operate flights to and from El Dorado, connecting Bogotá to destinations around the world.

Transport from the Airport:

- Taxi: Taxis are readily available at the airport. It is recommended to use authorized airport taxis for safety and convenience.
- Airport Shuttle: Some hotels provide airport shuttle services. Check with your accommodation for availability.

- Public Transportation: TransMilenio, Bogotá's rapid transit system, has a station at the airport, providing an economical way to reach the city center.

2. Land Travel: Bus Services and Terminals:

Overview:

- National Bus Terminals: Bogotá has several bus terminals, including Terminal de Transporte de Bogotá and Salitre Terminal, serving as hubs for long-distance buses from various regions of Colombia.
- Regional and Local Buses: Buses connect Bogotá with neighboring cities and towns. The city has an extensive network of public buses, including TransMilenio and SITP.

Transport from Regional Terminals:

- Taxi and Rideshare: Taxis and rideshare services are available at bus terminals for convenient transportation to your destination.
- Public Buses: TransMilenio feeder buses and SITP services provide connectivity to different parts of the city from regional terminals.

3. Car Travel: Roadways and Highways:

Overview:

- Road Network: Bogotá is connected to other cities and regions by a network of well-maintained highways. The city is accessible by car from various directions.
- Car Rentals: Rental car services are available at the airport and in the city center, offering flexibility for travelers who prefer driving.

Driving Tips:

- Traffic Conditions: Bogotá experiences traffic congestion, especially during peak hours. Plan your travel times accordingly.
- Parking: Secure parking facilities are available in the city. Some hotels also offer parking services.

4. Rail Travel:

Overview:

- Train Services: While Colombia is working on expanding its railway network, as of now, train services are limited, and there is no direct train connection to Bogotá.

5. Sea Travel: Ports and Cruises:

Overview:

- Sea Access: Bogotá is an inland city, and there are no direct sea routes to reach it. However, nearby coastal cities like Cartagena and Buenaventura have ports that can be accessed by sea.

Connecting from Coastal Cities:

- Domestic Flights: If arriving by sea to a coastal city, domestic flights are available to El Dorado International Airport in Bogotá.

Bogotá, as a major economic and cultural hub, is well-connected through a variety of transportation options. The choice of how to get to the city depends on your location, preferences, and the type of travel experience you seek. Whether you prefer the convenience of air travel, the scenic journey by road, or the regional charm of buses, Bogotá welcomes you with diverse options to start your Colombian adventure.

Navigating the City

Bogotá, a sprawling metropolis nestled in the Andes, offers a range of transportation options to navigate its diverse neighborhoods and vibrant districts. From public transit systems to taxis and cycling initiatives, here's an in-depth exploration of the various transportation modes available in Bogotá:

1. TransMilenio: Rapid Transit System:

Overview:

- Bus Rapid Transit: TransMilenio is Bogotá's highly efficient bus rapid transit system, known for its dedicated bus lanes and articulated buses.
- Corridors: The system operates on multiple corridors that crisscross the city, connecting various neighborhoods.
- Stations: TransMilenio stations are strategically located, making it a convenient mode of transportation for both locals and visitors.

How to Use:

- Fare System: TransMilenio uses a fare card system. Travelers need to purchase a card and load it with credits for trips.
- Feeder Buses: Feeder buses connect neighborhoods to TransMilenio stations, providing comprehensive coverage.

2. SITP: Integrated Public Transport System:

Overview:

- Comprehensive Network: The Sistema Integrado de Transporte Público (SITP) integrates buses into a unified public transportation system.
- Different Services: SITP includes various services, such as zonal buses, complementary services, and provisional routes.

How to Use:

- Payment Options: Similar to TransMilenio, SITP uses a smart card system for fare payment.
- Route Information: Clear route information and maps are available at stops and online for easy navigation.

3. Cycling: Bike Paths and Ciclovía:

Overview:

- Bike-Friendly City: Bogotá has been actively promoting cycling as a sustainable and healthy mode of transportation.
- Ciclovía: Every Sunday and public holiday, many major roads are closed to vehicular traffic, transforming into Ciclovía, a space for cyclists, joggers, and pedestrians.

How to Use:

- Bike Rentals: Bike rental services are available throughout the city, providing an accessible option for exploring Bogotá on two wheels.
- Bike Paths: Dedicated bike paths are present in many areas, enhancing safety for cyclists.

4. Taxis and Rideshare:

Overview:

- Abundant Taxis: Taxis are widely available throughout Bogotá and offer a convenient way to travel, especially in the evenings or areas with limited public transportation.
- Rideshare Apps: Apps like Uber and local alternatives provide an additional option for reliable and secure transportation.

How to Use:

- Metered Fare: Taxis in Bogotá operate on a metered fare system. Ensure the driver starts the meter at the beginning of your journey.
- App-Based Payment: Rideshare services usually have cashless transactions, making payments seamless.

5. Private Cars and Rental Services:

Overview:

- Car Rentals: Several international and local car rental agencies operate in Bogotá, providing flexibility for travelers who prefer to drive.
- Ride-Hailing Services: Apps like Uber also offer private car services for those who prefer a more personalized experience.

Driving Tips:

- Traffic Conditions: Bogotá experiences traffic congestion, particularly during rush hours. Plan travel times accordingly.
- Parking: Secure parking facilities are available, and some hotels offer parking services.

6. Walking:

Overview:

- Pedestrian-Friendly Areas: Bogotá has designated pedestrian-friendly areas, particularly in neighborhoods like La Candelaria, where walking is the best way to explore.

Tips:

- Comfortable Shoes: Wear comfortable shoes as you navigate the city on foot, especially in hilly areas.

Bogotá's transportation ecosystem provides a seamless blend of public and private options, allowing residents and visitors to move around the city efficiently. Whether you choose the speed of TransMilenio, the flexibility of cycling, or the convenience of taxis, navigating Bogotá is an accessible and enjoyable experience, revealing the city's vibrant culture and diverse neighborhoods at every turn.

Chapter 4

Accommodation Options

Bogotá, the vibrant capital of Colombia, offers a diverse range of accommodation options to suit every traveler's preferences, from the luxurious to the budget-friendly. Whether you seek the personalized charm of boutique hotels or the cost-effective comfort of budget accommodations, Bogotá has a plethora of choices. Here's a detailed exploration of the accommodation landscape in Bogotá, helping you find the perfect place to call home during your stay.

Luxury Stays in Bogotá

Bogotá, Colombia, offers an array of luxurious accommodations that cater to discerning travelers seeking opulence, top-notch service, and sophisticated amenities. From prestigious hotels in the heart of the financial district to charming retreats nestled in the city's cultural hubs, these luxury stays promise an unforgettable experience. Here's an in-depth exploration of recommended luxury accommodations and their captivating locations in Bogotá:

1. Four Seasons Hotel Casa Medina Bogotá:

Location: Carrera 7 #69A-22, Zona G

- Overview: Housed in a beautifully restored historic mansion, the Four Seasons Hotel Casa Medina Bogotá seamlessly blends colonial charm with modern luxury. The Zona G (Gourmet Zone) location puts you in the midst of Bogotá's upscale dining and shopping district.

Features:

- Exquisite rooms and suites with elegant decor and modern amenities.
- Gourmet dining options, including local and international cuisines.
- Spa facilities offering indulgent treatments and relaxation.
- Convenient access to cultural attractions and upscale boutiques.

2. JW Marriott Hotel Bogotá:

Location: Calle 73 #8-60

- Overview: Situated in the vibrant financial district of Bogotá, the JW Marriott Hotel offers a luxurious escape with its contemporary design and impeccable service. The location provides easy access to business centers, shopping, and cultural venues.

Features:

- Spacious and stylish rooms and suites with modern amenities.
- High-end dining options showcasing Colombian and international cuisine.
- Executive lounge for added exclusivity and personalized services.
- Proximity to entertainment venues and corporate offices.

3. Click Clack Hotel:

Location: Carrera 11 #93-77, Chapinero

- Overview: For those seeking a contemporary and eco-friendly luxury stay, the Click Clack Hotel in Chapinero offers a stylish retreat with a focus on sustainability. The location provides a vibrant atmosphere with trendy cafes, boutiques, and nightlife.

Features:

- Modern and eclectic rooms with unique design elements.
- Sustainable practices, including rainwater harvesting and energy efficiency.
- Rooftop terrace with panoramic city views and a lively bar scene.
- Proximity to the Zona G and Zona T for upscale dining and entertainment.

4. Casa Legado:

Location: Carrera 3 #12-86, La Candelaria

- Overview: Nestled in the heart of La Candelaria, Casa Legado is a luxury boutique hotel housed in a colonial-style mansion. The location immerses guests in the cultural richness of Bogotá's historic district.

Features:

- Individually decorated rooms with a blend of modern and antique furnishings.
- A tranquil courtyard garden and a rooftop terrace with city views.
- Personalized service and a focus on local art and culture.
- Proximity to landmarks like the Botero Museum and Teatro Colón.

5. Hotel de la Ópera:

Location: Calle 10 #5-72, La Candelaria

- Overview: Steeped in history, Hotel de la Ópera is a luxury hotel set in a colonial-style building in La Candelaria. The location provides a romantic and cultural retreat near historic sites and theaters.

Features:

- Elegant rooms and suites with classic decor and modern amenities.
- Fine dining restaurant with a focus on Colombian and Mediterranean cuisine.
- A courtyard with a fountain, creating a serene atmosphere.
- Proximity to cultural venues like the Teatro Colón and the Cathedral of Bogotá.

6. Casa Sanz:

Location: Calle 11 #2-38, La Candelaria

- Overview: Situated in the heart of La Candelaria, Casa Sanz is a boutique luxury hotel housed in a beautifully restored colonial building. The location provides a central and historic setting for exploring Bogotá's cultural gems.

Features:

- Stylish rooms and suites with a mix of colonial and contemporary design.
- A rooftop terrace with panoramic views of the city and Monserrate.
- Personalized service, including guided city tours and local insights.
- Proximity to landmarks like Plaza Bolívar and the Gold Museum.

7. Movich Buró 26:

Location: Calle 26B #103-18

- Overview: Perfectly situated for travelers in transit, Movich Buró 26 is located near El Dorado International Airport. This luxury hotel offers a comfortable and convenient stay with modern amenities and airport connectivity.

Features:

- Contemporary rooms and suites designed for relaxation and productivity.
- On-site dining options serving a variety of cuisines.
- Airport shuttle services for seamless transit.
- Proximity to the Corferias Convention Center and business districts.

Choosing one of these luxury stays in Bogotá ensures not only a lavish experience but also convenient access to the city's cultural, business, and entertainment hubs. Whether you prefer the historic charm of La Candelaria or the modern vibrancy of Chapinero, these accommodations promise an indulgent retreat in Colombia's bustling capital.

Boutique Stays in Bogotá

Bogotá, Colombia, boasts a vibrant boutique hotel scene, each offering a unique blend of charm, character, and personalized service. From historic districts to trendy neighborhoods, these boutique stays promise an intimate and memorable experience. Here's an in-depth exploration of some top boutique recommendations and their enchanting locations:

1. The Orchids Hotel:

Location: Carrera 5 #10-55, La Candelaria

- Overview: Tucked away in the historic La Candelaria neighborhood, The Orchids Hotel is a boutique gem known for its intimate atmosphere and attention to detail. The location immerses guests in the charm of colonial architecture and cultural landmarks.

Features:

- Boutique rooms and suites with unique decor and period furnishings.
- An intimate courtyard setting and a rooftop terrace with panoramic views.
- Personalized concierge services for tailored experiences.
- Proximity to attractions like Plaza Bolívar and the Gold Museum.

2. Casa Gaitán Cortés Bed & Breakfast:

Location: Calle 11 #3-11, La Candelaria

- Overview: This Bed & Breakfast in La Candelaria, Casa Gaitán Cortés, offers a personalized and local experience. Set in a traditional house, it provides cozy rooms, a courtyard garden, and a warm atmosphere. Guests can enjoy the proximity to landmarks like the Gold Museum and Plaza Bolívar.

3. Hotel de Leyendas:

Location: Carrera 3 #12-47, La Candelaria

- Overview: Hotel de Leyendas offers a unique boutique experience in La Candelaria, focusing on local legends and folklore. The hotel is set in a historic building with themed rooms, a courtyard, and a central location near landmarks like Plaza Bolívar and the Botero Museum.

4. Casa Platypus:

Location: Calle 16 #2-43, La Candelaria

- Overview: Casa Platypus is a boutique hostel located in the heart of La Candelaria. With a mix of dormitory and private rooms, it provides a cozy and artistic ambiance. Guests can enjoy the proximity to cultural attractions, cafes, and vibrant street art in the neighborhood.

5. Arche Noah Boutique Hostel:

Location: Carrera 3 #12d-83, La Candelaria

- Overview: Arche Noah Boutique Hostel, situated in La Candelaria, offers a boutique hostel experience with a focus on sustainability. The hostel features artistic decor, a rooftop terrace with city views, and a commitment to eco-friendly practices. It provides a unique and socially responsible stay in Bogotá.

Choosing a boutique stay in Bogotá ensures a personalized and culturally rich experience, whether you're exploring the historic streets of La Candelaria or enjoying the trendy vibes of Chapinero. Each of these top recommendations offers a distinctive atmosphere, reflecting the diverse and dynamic character of Colombia's capital.

Budget-Friendly Stays in Bogotá

Bogotá, Colombia, caters to budget-conscious travelers with a range of affordable and comfortable accommodation options. From hostels to budget hotels, these stays provide an opportunity to explore the city without breaking the bank. Here's an in-depth exploration of some top budget-friendly recommendations and their convenient locations:

1. Selina Bogotá:

Location: La Candelaria or Chapinero (multiple locations)

- Overview: Selina, a boutique hostel chain, offers budget-friendly options in both La Candelaria and Chapinero. With a mix of dorms and private rooms, Selina provides a social atmosphere, creative common spaces, and affordability. It's an ideal choice for travelers seeking a vibrant and economical stay.

2. Masaya Hostel:

Location: Calle 12C #2-36, La Candelaria

- Overview: Masaya Hostel in La Candelaria is a budget-friendly accommodation known for its artistic and bohemian vibe. The hostel offers dormitory and private rooms, communal spaces adorned with local artwork, and a central location close to landmarks like Plaza Bolívar and the Botero Museum.

3. Fernweh Photography Hostel:

Location: Calle 12C #2-18, La Candelaria

- Overview: For budget travelers with a passion for photography, Fernweh Photography Hostel in La Candelaria is an exciting choice. The hostel features affordable dorms and private rooms, a photography studio, and a cozy atmosphere. It's situated near cultural attractions and lively cafes.

4. Explora Hostels:

Location: Carrera 3 #12C-86, La Candelaria

- Overview: Explora Hostels in La Candelaria provides budget-friendly accommodations with a focus on community engagement. With dormitory-style rooms, communal areas for socializing, and organized activities, this hostel is a great option for solo travelers or those looking for a dynamic atmosphere.

5. Casa Bellavista Hostel:

Location: Carrera 2 #12-48, La Candelaria

- Overview: Nestled in La Candelaria, Casa Bellavista Hostel offers budget-friendly dorms and private rooms. The hostel features a rooftop terrace with panoramic city views, a communal kitchen, and a relaxed ambiance. It's conveniently situated for exploring the historic district.

6. Musicology Hostel:

Location: Carrera 3 #12c-97, La Candelaria

- Overview: Music enthusiasts will appreciate the budget-friendly accommodations at Musicology Hostel in La Candelaria. With dormitory options, musical instruments for guests, and a laid-back vibe, this hostel offers a unique and affordable stay in the heart of the historic district.

7. Alegria's Hostel:

Location: Calle 11 #3-43, La Candelaria

- Overview: Alegria's Hostel in La Candelaria provides budget-friendly dorms and private rooms with a cheerful and welcoming atmosphere. The hostel features colorful decor, a communal kitchen, and proximity to cultural landmarks and vibrant street life.

8. Hostal Sue Candelaria:

Location: Carrera 4 #11-55, La Candelaria

- Overview: Hostal Sue Candelaria offers affordable accommodations in La Candelaria, with dormitory and private room options. The hostel provides a cozy environment, a communal lounge, and easy access to attractions like the Gold Museum and Plaza Bolívar.

9. Cranky Croc Hostel:

Location: Calle 12d #3-46, La Candelaria

- Overview: Cranky Croc Hostel is a budget-friendly option in La Candelaria, known for its lively atmosphere and social events. With dormitory-style rooms, a communal bar, and a central location, this hostel is a favorite among budget

- **10. Colombia Hostel:**

Location: Calle 12D #3-46, La Candelaria

- Overview: Colombia Hostel is situated in the heart of La Candelaria and offers budget-friendly dorms and private rooms. The hostel features a communal kitchen, a rooftop terrace, and a sociable environment, making it an excellent choice for travelers on a budget.

Choosing one of these budget-friendly stays in Bogotá ensures an economical yet enjoyable experience, whether you're exploring the historic charm of La Candelaria or the dynamic vibes of Chapinero. These accommodations provide an excellent balance between affordability, comfort, and the opportunity to connect with fellow travelers.

Choosing the right accommodation in Bogotá depends on your preferences, budget, and the type of experience you seek. Whether you opt for the luxury of a boutique hotel, the social atmosphere of a hostel, or the charm of a local guesthouse, Bogotá's diverse accommodation options ensure a comfortable and enriching stay in Colombia's capital.

Chapter 5

Exploring Bogotá's Neighborhoods

Exploring La Candelaria

La Candelaria, nestled in the heart of Bogotá, is a district that pulsates with history, art, and cultural richness. Its cobblestone streets and colonial architecture create an enchanting atmosphere that transports visitors to the city's early days. Let's delve into the myriad facets of La Candelaria:

Historical Significance:

- Colonial Origins: La Candelaria is the oldest neighborhood in Bogotá, dating back to the city's founding in 1538. Its historic significance is evident in the well-preserved colonial architecture and landmarks.

Key Attractions:

- Plaza Bolívar: The central square of La Candelaria, Plaza Bolívar, is surrounded by iconic structures like the Cathedral Primada, the Capitolio Nacional, and the Palace of Justice. It's a gathering place, both for locals and tourists, hosting events and cultural activities.
- Botero Museum: Housed in a colonial mansion, this museum showcases the works of renowned Colombian artist Fernando Botero. The collection includes paintings and sculptures that exhibit Botero's distinctive style of exaggerated forms.
- Gold Museum (Museo del Oro): A must-visit for history enthusiasts, the Gold Museum boasts an extensive

collection of pre-Columbian gold artifacts. It provides insights into the indigenous cultures that thrived in Colombia before the arrival of the Spanish.

- Chorro de Quevedo: Regarded as the birthplace of Bogotá, this historic square is a vibrant gathering spot. It is often bustling with street performers, artisans, and locals enjoying the lively atmosphere.

Architectural Delights:

- Colonial Houses: Wander through narrow streets lined with well-preserved colonial houses, each telling a story of Bogotá's past. Many of these historic homes have been converted into museums, art galleries, and boutique hotels.
- Church of San Francisco: A masterpiece of colonial architecture, this church dates back to the 16th century. Its intricate design and religious significance make it a captivating stop for those exploring La Candelaria.

Cultural Immersion:

- Street Art and Murals: La Candelaria is a canvas for urban expression, adorned with vibrant street art and murals. Take a leisurely stroll through the neighborhood to appreciate the creativity and messages conveyed through these artworks.
- Local Cafes and Restaurants: Embrace the local flavor by indulging in traditional Colombian cuisine at one of the neighborhood's many cafes and restaurants. These establishments often feature live music and a cozy ambiance.

Educational Institutions:

- Universidad de los Andes: La Candelaria is home to the prestigious Universidad de los Andes, adding an intellectual and youthful energy to the neighborhood. The university's campus features a mix of modern and historic buildings.

Cultural Events and Festivals:

- Cultural Calendar: La Candelaria hosts various cultural events, including music festivals, art exhibitions, and theater performances. The neighborhood comes alive with energy during these festivities, attracting locals and visitors alike.

Local Markets:

- Paloquemao Market: While not directly in La Candelaria, Paloquemao Market is a short distance away. It's a bustling market where you can experience the daily life of Bogotá's residents, sample fresh produce, and soak in the local atmosphere.

Tips for Exploration:

- Comfortable Footwear: The cobblestone streets can be uneven, so comfortable footwear is advisable for exploring the neighborhood on foot.

Guided Tours: Consider joining a guided walking tour to gain deeper insights into the history and stories behind La Candelaria's landmarks.

La Candelaria is not merely a neighborhood; it's a living testament to Bogotá's evolution, encapsulating centuries of history within its charming streets and architectural wonders. Whether you're captivated by its colonial houses, intrigued by its museums, or enchanted by its vibrant street life, La Candelaria offers an immersive and enriching experience for all who venture into its storied lanes.

Exploring Chapinero

Chapinero, a dynamic neighborhood in Bogotá, stands out as a hub of creativity, gastronomy, and vibrant nightlife. Its trendy atmosphere, diverse culinary scene, and lively entertainment options make it a must-visit for those seeking contemporary urban experiences. Let's delve into the allure of Chapinero:

Trendy Cafés and Culinary Scene:

Zona G (Gourmet Zone):

- Gastronomic Haven: Zona G is synonymous with culinary excellence, boasting a concentration of upscale restaurants, trendy cafes, and gourmet experiences. It's a paradise for food enthusiasts seeking a diverse range of international cuisines.
- Artisanal Delights: Explore artisanal bakeries, specialty coffee shops, and patisseries that grace the streets of Zona G. Each establishment brings a unique flavor to Bogotá's culinary landscape.

Zona T (Zona Rosa):

- Nightlife Hub: While known for its nightlife, Zona T is also home to chic cafes and restaurants. During the day, trendy cafés beckon patrons with aromatic Colombian coffee and delectable pastries.
- Gourmet Exploration: Zona T's daytime ambiance transforms seamlessly into a lively nightlife scene. After

enjoying a leisurely coffee, explore the gourmet restaurants that come alive in the evening.

Café Culture and Independent Bookstores:

- Café Hopping: Chapinero encourages a laid-back café culture, where locals and visitors alike can be found enjoying coffee in cozy settings. Trendy coffee shops often feature specialty brews and artistic atmospheres.
- Independent Bookstores: Interspersed among the cafés are independent bookstores, providing a haven for literary enthusiasts. These bookshops often host cultural events, readings, and discussions, adding an intellectual flair to the neighborhood.

Street Art and Murals:

- Urban Art Scene: Chapinero boasts a vibrant street art scene, with colorful murals adorning building facades. Take a self-guided tour to discover the diverse expressions of local and international artists that contribute to the neighborhood's artistic vibe.

Boutique Shopping and Cultural Spaces:

Boutique Shopping in Chapinero Alto:

- Chapinero Alto: This upscale section of Chapinero is known for its boutique shops and designer stores. Fashion enthusiasts can explore a mix of local and international brands, adding a touch of style to the neighborhood.
- Cultural Spaces: Amidst the shopping, discover cultural spaces that feature art galleries, performance venues, and independent theaters. These spaces contribute to the neighborhood's creative energy.

Safety and Accessibility:

- Nightlife Safety: Chapinero is renowned for its nightlife, and safety is a priority. Popular nightlife areas are well-patrolled, ensuring a secure environment for those exploring the city after dark.
- Public Transportation: The neighborhood's accessibility is enhanced by an efficient public transportation system. Buses and TransMilenio, Bogotá's rapid transit system, make it easy to navigate Chapinero and reach other parts of the city.

Cultural Events and Festivals:

- Festival Estéreo Picnic: Chapinero often hosts cultural events and festivals, such as the Festival Estéreo Picnic, a renowned music festival that attracts international and local artists. The neighborhood comes alive with music, art, and cultural celebrations during such events.

Nightlife Hotspots:

Andrés Carne de Res:

- Iconic Nightclub: Andrés Carne de Res is an iconic Bogotá nightclub located in Chapinero. Known for its lively atmosphere, eclectic decor, and diverse music, it's a must-visit for those seeking a memorable night out.

El Chorro de Quevedo:

- Historical Pub Hub: El Chorro de Quevedo, while historically significant, transforms into a lively pub hub at night. It's a popular spot for both locals and tourists to enjoy drinks and soak in the vibrant ambiance.

Tips for Exploration:

- Day-to-Night Transition: Experience the seamless transition of Chapinero from daytime cafés to nighttime hotspots. Start with a leisurely coffee and witness the neighborhood transform into a buzzing nightlife scene.
- Exploration on Foot: Chapinero is best explored on foot, allowing you to discover hidden gems, street art, and the unique charm of each café or cultural space.

Chapinero is a testament to Bogotá's ability to seamlessly blend tradition with modernity. From the trendy cafés and gourmet experiences of Zona G to the energetic nightlife of Zona T, this neighborhood invites you to immerse yourself in its dynamic cultural tapestry.

Exploring Usaquén

Usaquén, nestled in the northern part of Bogotá, stands out as a unique and charming neighborhood with a village-like atmosphere. Known for its cobbled streets, colonial architecture, and a thriving artistic community, Usaquén invites visitors to experience a blend of history, art, and culinary delights.

Quaint Markets:

Usaquén Square:

- Heart of the Neighborhood: Usaquén Square is the central gathering place, surrounded by cafes, restaurants, and artisanal shops. The square is a bustling hub, particularly on weekends when it hosts a renowned flea market.
- Sunday Flea Market: The Sunday flea market is a highlight, featuring stalls with handmade crafts, antiques, and

artisanal products. It's a perfect spot to immerse yourself in the local atmosphere and discover unique treasures.

Hacienda Santa Bárbara:

- Historic Shopping Center: Hacienda Santa Bárbara is a historic building turned shopping center in Usaquén. It houses a mix of boutiques, art galleries, and cafes, providing a delightful shopping experience in a colonial setting.

Artistic Vibes:

Art Galleries and Studios:

- Thriving Art Community: Usaquén has a vibrant artistic community, evident in the numerous art galleries and studios scattered throughout the neighborhood. Explore these spaces to discover the works of both local and international artists.
- Art Walks: Take leisurely art walks through Usaquén's streets, where murals, sculptures, and installations contribute to the neighborhood's artistic charm. Many artists find inspiration in Usaquén's unique ambiance.

Cultural Events:

- Usaquén Art Walk: The neighborhood occasionally hosts events like the Usaquén Art Walk, where artists showcase their works in open-air exhibitions. It's an opportunity to engage with the creative energy that permeates the streets.

Dining Experiences:

Culinary Diversity:

- International and Local Flavors: Usaquén's dining scene is diverse, offering a mix of international and local cuisines. From charming cafes to upscale restaurants, the neighborhood is a gastronomic delight.
- Al Fresco Dining: Many establishments feature al fresco dining options, allowing visitors to savor their meals while enjoying the picturesque surroundings of Usaquén's streets.

Parks and Green Spaces:

Parque de Usaquén:

- Tranquil Oasis: Parque de Usaquén is a green oasis in the midst of the urban landscape. It provides a serene setting for relaxation, picnics, and enjoying the outdoors.
- Public Events: The park is often a venue for public events, cultural performances, and local festivals, creating a dynamic and inclusive community space.

Architectural Delights:

Colonial Houses and Streets:

- Charming Architecture: Usaquén is characterized by well-preserved colonial houses with colorful facades and balconies. The streets, adorned with cobblestones, add to the neighborhood's historic charm.
- Historical Church: The Church of Santa Bárbara, located in Usaquén, is a colonial-era church with a simple yet elegant design. It adds a touch of historical significance to the neighborhood.

Local Experiences:

Traditional Craft Shops:

- Craftsmanship on Display: Usaquén is home to traditional craft shops where artisans showcase their handmade products. It's an ideal place to pick up unique souvenirs and support local craftsmanship.
- Interaction with Artisans: Some craft shops allow visitors to interact with artisans, providing insights into the creative processes behind the handmade items.

Tips for Exploration:

- Weekend Visit: Consider planning your visit to Usaquén on the weekend to experience the lively atmosphere of the Sunday flea market and the various cultural events that often take place.
- Exploration on Foot: Usaquén's charm is best explored on foot. Take leisurely strolls through its streets, discovering hidden gems, art installations, and quaint corners.

Usaquén invites you to step into a world where history and creativity converge. Whether you're exploring the vibrant markets, engaging with local artists, or savoring diverse flavors in charming cafes, this neighborhood offers a captivating escape from the bustling city, creating a lasting impression of Bogotá's cultural richness.

Chapter 6

Outdoor Escapades and Nature Retreats

Monserrate: Hiking the Iconic Bogotá Peak

Monserrate, a towering peak that overlooks Bogotá, is more than just a geographical landmark; it's a symbol of the city's spiritual and natural essence. Ascending Monserrate is not merely a hike; it's a journey that offers breathtaking views, cultural experiences, and a profound connection with nature. Let's explore the outdoor escapades and nature retreats associated with this iconic peak.

Hiking Adventure:

Trail Options:

- Piedras del Tunjo Trail: This is the most common hiking trail, known for its accessibility. The trail winds through lush greenery, providing glimpses of Bogotá below.
- Old Train Track Trail: For those seeking a historical touch, the old train track trail offers a scenic route with remnants of the historic railway.

Difficulty Levels:

- Beginner-Friendly: The Piedras del Tunjo trail is suitable for beginners, with well-maintained paths and moderate inclines.
- Intermediate to Advanced: For a more challenging hike, the Old Train Track trail presents steeper sections and a longer trek.

Cultural and Spiritual Exploration:

Monserrate Sanctuary:

- Religious Significance: At the summit, you'll find the Santuario de Monserrate, a pilgrimage site with a centuries-old history. Pilgrims climb the peak seeking spiritual fulfillment and to pay homage to El Señor Caído (the Fallen Lord).
- Religious Festivals: The sanctuary hosts religious festivals, providing an opportunity to witness traditional rituals and experience the cultural vibrancy associated with Monserrate.

Panoramic Views:

Cityscape Vista:

- Breathtaking Panorama: The summit of Monserrate offers an unparalleled panoramic view of Bogotá. The cityscape stretches as far as the eye can see, providing a unique perspective of the capital nestled within the Andean mountains.
- Day and Night Views: Whether you embark on the hike during the day or opt for a nighttime visit, the views from the top are equally mesmerizing. The city lights create a spectacular spectacle after sunset.

Nature Retreats:

Biodiversity and Flora:

- Andean Ecosystem: As you ascend Monserrate, you'll traverse through diverse ecosystems, from cloud forests to high-altitude shrublands. The journey allows you to observe Andean flora and fauna, including unique plant species and birdlife.

- Botanical Interest: Botanists and nature enthusiasts will appreciate the variety of endemic plants, some of which are specific to the high-altitude environment.

Alternative Modes of Transportation:

Cable Car and Funicular:

- Scenic Rides: For those preferring a less strenuous ascent, Monserrate offers both a cable car and a funicular railway. These options provide a scenic ride with panoramic views, allowing visitors to experience the beauty of Monserrate with ease.
- Convenient Access: The cable car and funicular depart from the base of the mountain, providing convenient access for visitors with various mobility levels.

Culinary Experiences:

Summit Dining:

- Gastronomic Delights: The summit of Monserrate is home to restaurants serving Colombian cuisine. Enjoy local delicacies while savoring the spectacular backdrop of Bogotá below.
- Altitude-Influenced Dishes: Some eateries offer dishes prepared with ingredients that thrive at higher altitudes, providing a unique culinary experience.

Tips for Hiking Monserrate:

- Comfortable Footwear: Wear comfortable hiking shoes suitable for variable terrain.
- Hydration: Carry sufficient water, especially if opting for the hiking trails.

- Sun Protection: Use sunscreen and wear a hat to protect against the Andean sun.
- Weather Awareness: Be prepared for changing weather conditions; Bogotá's altitude can result in cooler temperatures.

Monserrate is not just a mountain; it's a multifaceted experience encompassing outdoor adventure, cultural exploration, and communion with nature. Whether you choose to hike, take the cable car, or explore the cultural aspects, a visit to Monserrate is an immersive journey that offers a profound connection to the natural and spiritual essence of Bogotá.

Ciclovía: Biking Through Bogotá's Car-Free Sundays

Ciclovía, a beloved tradition in Bogotá, transforms the cityscape into a vibrant tapestry of cyclists, joggers, and pedestrians every Sunday and public holiday. This car-free initiative has become an integral part of Bogotá's culture, offering outdoor enthusiasts and families a unique way to explore the city's streets, parks, and cultural landmarks. Let's dive into the details of this outdoor escapade and nature retreat:

Car-Free Streets:

Citywide Route:

- Extensive Network: Ciclovía spans over 120 kilometers of car-free routes, connecting various neighborhoods and cultural landmarks. The streets are closed to vehicular traffic, allowing residents and visitors to reclaim the roadways for recreational activities.
- Sunday Tradition: Every Sunday and public holiday, from 7 a.m. to 2 p.m., Bogotá's major roads transform into a

cyclist's paradise, creating a sense of community and shared public spaces.

Cycling Adventures:

Bike Rentals and Stations:

- Accessibility: For those without a bike, numerous bike rental stations are available along the Ciclovía route. This ensures accessibility for individuals of all ages and backgrounds.
- Variety of Bikes: Rental options include traditional bikes, tandems, and even specialized bikes for children, making it a family-friendly activity.

Scenic Landmarks and Parks:

Cultural and Historical Stops:

- Landmark Exploration: Ciclovía allows cyclists to explore Bogotá's cultural and historical landmarks at a leisurely pace. Cyclists can stop at iconic sites such as Plaza de Bolívar, Bogotá's main square, and marvel at the city's architectural heritage.
- Museums and Galleries: Many museums and galleries along the route open their doors to the public during Ciclovía, providing an opportunity for cultural enrichment.

Green Spaces:

- Parque Nacional: This expansive urban park along the Ciclovía route offers lush greenery, recreational spaces, and a serene environment for picnics or relaxation.
- Simon Bolivar Metropolitan Park: One of the largest urban parks in Bogotá, it provides a scenic backdrop for cyclists,

joggers, and families looking to enjoy nature within the city.

Fitness and Wellness Activities:

Open-Air Exercise Classes:

- Fitness Opportunities: Ciclovía isn't just about cycling; it's a holistic wellness experience. Along the route, participants can join open-air exercise classes, including yoga, aerobics, and dance sessions.
- Community Engagement: The open-air classes foster a sense of community, bringing together individuals with a shared interest in health and well-being.

Culinary and Artisan Experiences:

Street Food and Markets:

- Culinary Delights: Ciclovía is not just about physical activity; it's a feast for the senses. Numerous food stalls and markets line the route, offering a diverse range of Colombian street food and artisanal products.
- Local Artisans: Engage with local artisans who showcase their crafts along the route, providing a unique opportunity to purchase handmade souvenirs and support local entrepreneurship.

Community Engagement:

Inclusive Activities:

- Accessible to All: Ciclovía is inclusive and caters to people of all ages and fitness levels. Families with children, seniors, and individuals with varying abilities can participate in the activities, fostering a sense of unity and inclusivity.

- Community Events: The car-free Sundays often feature community events, cultural performances, and live music, creating a festive and celebratory atmosphere.

Tips for Ciclovía Exploration:

- Comfortable Attire: Wear comfortable clothing suitable for cycling or outdoor activities.
- Hydration: Bring water to stay hydrated, especially in Bogotá's high-altitude environment.
- Sun Protection: Apply sunscreen and wear sunglasses to protect against the sun.
- Explore Beyond Biking: While cycling is a highlight, consider exploring other activities, such as yoga classes or cultural stops.

Ciclovía is not just an outdoor escapade; it's a celebration of community, culture, and well-being. Biking through Bogotá's car-free Sundays allows participants to connect with the city in a unique way, fostering a sense of shared public spaces and promoting a healthy and active lifestyle. Whether you're a seasoned cyclist or a casual participant, Ciclovía offers an unforgettable experience of Bogotá's streets and culture.

Salt Cathedral of Zipaquirá: A Subterranean Wonder

Nestled deep within the Andean mountains, the Salt Cathedral of Zipaquirá stands as a testament to human ingenuity and spiritual devotion. This subterranean marvel, located just outside Bogotá, Colombia, is a breathtaking fusion of art, architecture, and natural wonders. Let's explore in detail the outdoor escapades and nature retreats offered by this extraordinary underground cathedral.

Journey to Zipaquirá:

Scenic Drive:

- Andean Landscape: The journey to the Salt Cathedral involves a scenic drive through the Andean mountains, offering panoramic views of the Colombian countryside. The route itself is an outdoor adventure, with winding roads and glimpses of rural life.
- Day Trip Possibility: Zipaquirá is easily accessible from Bogotá, making it a perfect day trip for those seeking a blend of natural beauty and cultural exploration.

Subterranean Architecture:

Cathedral Chambers:

- Salt Carved Interiors: The Salt Cathedral is not just a place of worship; it's an architectural masterpiece carved out of the salt deposits within the mountains. Each chamber tells a story through intricate salt sculptures, creating an otherworldly atmosphere.
- Cathedral Layout: The cathedral is divided into three sections representing the birth, life, and death of Jesus. Each section features awe-inspiring salt-carved sculptures, including the monumental cross in the central nave.

Cultural and Spiritual Exploration:

Religious Significance:

- Pilgrimage Destination: The Salt Cathedral is a pilgrimage destination for many, attracting visitors seeking both religious contemplation and a unique cultural experience.

- Stations of the Cross: The cathedral features stations of the cross, each carved from salt, creating a spiritual journey for visitors as they move through the underground chambers.

Natural Wonders:

Halite Chambers:

- Halite Formation: Halite, the mineral form of sodium chloride (salt), dominates the chambers of the cathedral. Visitors can witness the natural beauty of salt formations, adding an element of geological wonder to the experience.
- Play of Light: Ingenious lighting designs enhance the natural beauty of the salt formations, creating a mesmerizing play of light and shadow within the subterranean space.

Outdoor Plaza and Views:

Plaza de las Minas:

- Open-Air Plaza: The exterior of the Salt Cathedral features the Plaza de las Minas, an open-air space where visitors can enjoy panoramic views of the surrounding landscape.
- Andean Scenery: The outdoor plaza provides an opportunity to breathe in the crisp mountain air and appreciate the Andean scenery, creating a harmonious balance between the subterranean wonders and the natural landscape.

Guided Tours and Interpretation:

Multilingual Guides:

- In-Depth Interpretation: Guided tours are available in multiple languages, offering visitors in-depth insights into the history, architecture, and cultural significance of the Salt Cathedral.

- Interactive Experience: Some tours provide interactive elements, allowing visitors to actively engage with the cathedral's history and symbolism.

Accessibility and Safety:

Climbing to the Cross:

- Climbing Experience: For the adventurous, there's an option to climb to the top of the Salt Cathedral, reaching the monumental cross that stands as a beacon within the cavernous space.
- Safety Measures: The cathedral is equipped with safety features to ensure a secure and enjoyable experience for visitors of all ages.

Tips for Exploration:

- Comfortable Attire: Wear comfortable clothing and footwear suitable for walking and mild temperatures within the underground environment.
- Photography: Capture the mesmerizing salt-carved sculptures and the interplay of light and shadow, but be mindful of any photography restrictions.
- Climbing Considerations: If considering the climb to the cross, assess your physical fitness and ensure it aligns with the experience.

The Salt Cathedral of Zipaquirá is not just a destination; it's a sublime blend of nature, culture, and spirituality. Exploring this subterranean wonder provides an opportunity for outdoor escapades, cultural enrichment, and a deep connection with the natural wonders hidden within the Andean mountains. Whether you're drawn by religious curiosity, architectural marvels, or the geological beauty of salt formations, the Salt Cathedral offers an unforgettable journey beneath the surface of Colombia's rich cultural and natural heritage.

Parque Nacional: Urban Oasis for Outdoor Enthusiasts

- Green Respite: Parque Nacional, located in the heart of Bogotá, offers a serene escape with lush greenery, walking paths, and open spaces for picnics and relaxation.
- Outdoor Workouts: Join locals engaged in various outdoor activities, from jogging and yoga to group fitness classes. The park's ambiance encourages a healthy and active lifestyle.
- Cultural Stops: Discover cultural attractions within the park, including sculptures, fountains, and occasional art exhibitions, adding an artistic touch to your outdoor experience.

Guatavita Lake: Kayaking Amidst Scenic Landscapes

- Day Trip Excursion: Head to Guatavita Lake, a short drive from Bogotá, for a day of kayaking in the pristine mountain surroundings. The lake's calm waters provide an ideal setting for water adventures.
- Scenic Beauty: Paddle through the lake's crystal-clear waters surrounded by lush greenery and picturesque landscapes. The experience offers a tranquil escape from the bustling city.

- Cultural Connection: Learn about the indigenous Muisca people and the legend of El Dorado associated with the lake. Explore the nearby town of Guatavita for a cultural immersion.

Rock Climbing in Suesca: Thrills on Natural Rocks

- Rock Climbing Hub: Suesca, a short drive from Bogotá, is a renowned rock climbing destination with natural rock formations. Engage in thrilling rock-climbing experiences suitable for all skill levels.
- Guided Adventures: Join guided rock-climbing excursions led by experienced instructors who ensure safety and provide insights into the geological features of the rocks.
- Breathtaking Views: As you ascend the rock faces, enjoy breathtaking views of the surrounding countryside, creating a memorable blend of adrenaline and natural beauty.

La Chorrera Waterfall: A Cascading Nature Retreat

- Trek Through Nature: Experience a nature retreat by hiking to La Chorrera, Colombia's tallest waterfall. The trek takes you through cloud forests, offering glimpses of diverse flora and fauna.
- Waterfall Majesty: Reach the majestic La Chorrera, where water cascades from a height of over 500 meters. The sight and sound of the waterfall create a serene atmosphere, perfect for nature enthusiasts.
- Picnic and Relaxation: Pack a picnic and unwind in the natural surroundings, absorbing the tranquility of the waterfall and its pristine environment.

Tips for Outdoor Adventures in Bogotá:

- Weather Awareness: Bogotá's climate can vary, so dress in layers and be prepared for changing conditions, especially at higher altitudes.
- Hydration: Carry water to stay hydrated, especially during outdoor activities like hiking and cycling.
- Local Guidance: For certain adventures, consider joining guided tours or hiring local experts to enhance your experience and ensure safety.
- Sun Protection: Apply sunscreen and wear appropriate sun protection, given Bogotá's high-altitude sun.

Bogotá's outdoor adventures promise a dynamic blend of cultural exploration, natural wonders, and adrenaline-fueled activities. Whether you're scaling the heights of Monserrate, cycling through car-free streets, or kayaking on scenic lakes, Bogotá invites you to embrace the thrill of the outdoors amidst the cultural richness of Colombia's capital city.

Chapter 7

Day Trips from Bogotá

Villa de Leyva: Colonial Charm and Fossils

Nestled in the Andean highlands, just a few hours from Bogotá, Villa de Leyva stands as a well-preserved colonial town with a captivating blend of history, architecture, and natural wonders. A day trip to Villa de Leyva promises a journey back in time as you wander through cobbled streets, explore colonial landmarks, and delve into the paleontological treasures that make this town a unique destination.

Colonial Architectural Marvels:

- Plaza Mayor: Begin your exploration at Plaza Mayor, one of the largest town squares in South America. Encircled by colonial-era buildings with white facades and wooden balconies, the plaza exudes a timeless charm.
- Casa Terracota: Marvel at Casa Terracota, a remarkable structure made entirely of clay. This modern architectural masterpiece stands out amidst the colonial backdrop, offering a unique blend of traditional and contemporary design.

Historical and Cultural Exploration:

- Iglesia Parroquial: Visit the Iglesia Parroquial, a Baroque-style church on the Plaza Mayor. Dating back to the 17th century, its grand facade and interior showcase the religious and architectural heritage of Villa de Leyva.

- Museo del Carmen: Immerse yourself in the local culture at the Museo del Carmen, located in a colonial-era convent. The museum houses religious artifacts, artwork, and historical exhibits, providing insights into the town's cultural evolution.

Paleontological Wonders:

- El Fósil Museum: Delve into the prehistoric world at El Fósil Museum, renowned for its collection of fossils. Admire the well-preserved remains of marine creatures and giant reptiles, including the spectacular Kronosaurus.
- Fossil-Hunting Tour: For a hands-on experience, consider joining a guided fossil-hunting tour to nearby sites. Skilled guides share insights into the region's geological history, allowing you to discover fossils hidden beneath the earth.

Natural Beauty and Outdoor Activities:

- Pozo Azul: Enjoy a moment of tranquility at Pozo Azul, a natural pool surrounded by lush vegetation. Whether you choose to swim or simply relax by the water, Pozo Azul offers a refreshing break.
- La Periquera Waterfalls: Embark on a short hike to La Periquera Waterfalls, where the natural beauty of cascading water amidst scenic landscapes provides a perfect setting for exploration and adventure.

Gastronomic Delights:

- Local Cuisine: Indulge in the flavors of Colombian cuisine at one of Villa de Leyva's charming restaurants. Sample regional dishes, and perhaps try the local specialty, "ajiaco," a hearty soup.

- Artisanal Markets: Explore the town's artisanal markets, where you can find locally crafted souvenirs and treats. These markets are perfect for discovering unique items to take home as reminders of your day trip.

Tips for Your Day Trip:

- Comfortable Attire: Wear comfortable shoes suitable for walking on cobblestone streets, and dress in layers to adapt to changes in weather.
- Local Guided Tours: Consider joining a guided tour to gain deeper insights into the town's history, culture, and geological wonders.
- Photography Essentials: Bring a camera to capture the architectural details, landscapes, and unique experiences throughout your day in Villa de Leyva.
- Local Events: Check for any local events or festivals happening during your visit to enhance your cultural experience.

Villa de Leyva, with its colonial charm and fossil-rich history, provides a captivating day trip from Bogotá. Whether you're immersed in the town's architectural legacy, exploring paleontological wonders, or savoring the local flavors, Villa de Leyva invites you to step into a world where the past and present coexist in harmony.

Guatavita: Legends of the El Dorado Lagoon

Embark on a captivating day trip from Bogotá to Guatavita, a town steeped in indigenous history and famous for the mythical El Dorado ceremony. Guatavita and its mystical lagoon have played a significant role in the cultural and historical tapestry of Colombia.

Join this journey to explore the legends, the town's unique charm, and the enigmatic Guatavita Lake.

1. Guatavita Town Exploration:

- Plaza Principal: Start your exploration at Plaza Principal, the heart of Guatavita. This picturesque square is surrounded by colonial-style buildings, creating a tranquil atmosphere. Take a leisurely stroll and absorb the ambiance of this historic town.

- Casa Cultural de Guatavita: Dive into the cultural heritage of Guatavita at Casa Cultural de Guatavita. This cultural center showcases indigenous art, artifacts, and exhibits that provide insights into the history and traditions of the Muisca people, the indigenous group associated with the El Dorado legend.

2. Guatavita Lake and El Dorado Legend:

- Guatavita Lake: Journey to the iconic Guatavita Lake, the setting for the legendary El Dorado ritual. Surrounded by lush landscapes, the lake holds a mysterious allure. Learn about the rituals conducted by the Muisca people and the significance of this sacred site.

- Legend of El Dorado: Unravel the fascinating legend of El Dorado, a mythical ceremony where indigenous leaders covered themselves in gold dust before making offerings to the gods in the middle of Guatavita Lake. The legend of El Dorado has captured the imaginations of explorers and storytellers for centuries.

3. Hiking Trails and Nature Walks:

- Scenic Hiking Trails: Explore the natural beauty surrounding Guatavita Lake by taking one of the scenic hiking trails. These trails offer breathtaking views of the lake and the lush Andean landscape. Choose a trail that suits your preferences, whether you're looking for a short nature walk or a more challenging hike.
- Bird Watching: Guatavita's natural surroundings are home to diverse bird species. Bring binoculars and enjoy bird watching as you meander through the trails. The serene environment provides an ideal setting for observing local birdlife.

4. Gastronomic Exploration:

- Local Cuisine: Indulge in local flavors at one of Guatavita's charming restaurants. Sample traditional Colombian dishes and savor the culinary delights that the town has to offer. The local cuisine often reflects the rich agricultural traditions of the region.

5. Handicraft Markets:

- Artisanal Souvenirs: Explore the artisanal markets in Guatavita, where you can find handmade crafts and souvenirs. Support local artisans and take home a piece of Guatavita's cultural heritage, from intricately crafted textiles to indigenous-inspired artwork.

Tips for Your Day Trip:

- Comfortable Attire: Wear comfortable clothing and sturdy shoes, especially if you plan to explore hiking trails or walk around the lake.

- Guided Tours: Consider joining a guided tour to Guatavita to gain deeper insights into the history, legends, and cultural significance of the town and its surroundings.
- Sun Protection: Given the high-altitude location, apply sunscreen, wear a hat, and bring sunglasses to protect yourself from the sun.
- Camera and Binoculars: Capture the beauty of Guatavita's landscapes and the cultural experience, and bring binoculars for bird watching.

Guatavita, with its legends of El Dorado and serene lake, offers a day trip filled with cultural exploration and natural beauty. Whether you're drawn to the mystique of the El Dorado legend, the scenic landscapes, or the vibrant culture of the town, Guatavita invites you to step into a world where history and mythology converge in a breathtaking Andean setting.

Zipaquirá: Beyond the Salt Cathedral

Just a short journey from Bogotá lies Zipaquirá, a town renowned for its iconic Salt Cathedral. However, Zipaquirá offers more than its subterranean wonder. This day trip invites you to explore the town's historical and cultural richness, lush natural surroundings, and engage in outdoor activities beyond the salt mines.

1. Zipaquirá's Historic Center:

Plaza de los Comuneros: Start your day by exploring the heart of Zipaquirá at Plaza de los Comuneros. This charming square is surrounded by colonial architecture, including the Cathedral Basilica of the Lord of the Miracles.

Catedral Basílica Metropolitana del Señor de los Milagros: Visit the Cathedral Basilica, a masterpiece of Gothic Revival architecture. The intricate details of its interior and the religious significance make it a must-visit cultural and historical site.

2. Zipaquirá's Local Markets:

Plaza de Mercado: Immerse yourself in the local culture by wandering through Plaza de Mercado. This bustling market offers a vibrant array of fresh produce, artisanal goods, and local crafts. Engage with locals and savor the authentic atmosphere.

3. Salt Cathedral Exploration:

Salt Cathedral Tour: While the Salt Cathedral is the town's most famous attraction, delve deeper into its chambers and tunnels. Learn about the salt mining history, religious significance, and marvel at the mesmerizing salt-carved sculptures and architecture.

4. Outdoor Escapades:

Parque de la Sal: After exploring the depths of the salt mines, unwind at Parque de la Sal. This park offers green spaces, walking trails, and recreational areas. It's an ideal spot for a leisurely stroll or a picnic amid the natural surroundings.

5. Adventure at Parque Jaime Duque:

Parque Jaime Duque: Extend your day trip by heading to Parque Jaime Duque, located near Zipaquirá. This amusement and wildlife park features replicas of world landmarks, a botanical garden, and a zoo. It's a perfect family-friendly destination.

6. Guatavita Lake Excursion:

Guatavita Lake: For a serene experience, take a short drive to Guatavita Lake. Nestled in the Andean highlands, this lake is surrounded by lush landscapes. Enjoy a boat ride or hike around the lake, absorbing the tranquility of the natural environment.

7. Culinary Delights:

Local Restaurants: Explore Zipaquirá's culinary scene by dining in local restaurants. Sample traditional Colombian dishes, and don't miss the opportunity to try "agua de panela con queso," a local beverage made from sugarcane and cheese.

Tips for Your Day Trip:

- Comfortable Attire: Wear comfortable clothing and footwear suitable for walking, especially if you plan to explore outdoor areas.
- Local Guides: Consider hiring a local guide to provide insights into Zipaquirá's history, culture, and lesser-known attractions.
- Sun Protection: Given the high-altitude location, apply sunscreen and wear a hat to protect yourself from the sun.
- Souvenirs: Support local artisans by purchasing souvenirs from the markets, adding a touch of Zipaquirá to your memories.

A day trip to Zipaquirá offers a rich tapestry of history, culture, and outdoor experiences beyond the famous Salt Cathedral. Whether you're captivated by the town's historic center, exploring local markets, or enjoying the natural beauty of Guatavita Lake, Zipaquirá invites you to uncover its multifaceted charm.

Chapter 8

Nightlife and Entertainment

Bogotá Nightlife and Entertainment Hotspots

1. Zona T: The Heart of Bogotá's Nightlife

Location: Calle 82 #12-52

Zona T, nestled in the upscale Chapinero district, is the pulsating heart of Bogotá's nightlife. This dynamic area offers a plethora of entertainment options, from trendy bars to high-energy clubs. Let's explore some top recommendations:

a. Theatron: World's Largest Gay Club

Location: Calle 58 #10-32

- Highlights: With 13 different themed rooms and a capacity for thousands, Theatron is a must-visit for an unparalleled clubbing experience. Each room offers a unique atmosphere and music genre, making it one of the most diverse nightlife venues in the world.

b. Andrés DC: Colombian Culinary and Party Fusion

Location: Carrera 13 #82-47

- Highlights: Andrés DC is a fusion of restaurant and nightclub, offering a vibrant atmosphere with Colombian folklore, delicious cuisine, and an energetic dance floor. The décor mirrors Colombian traditions, creating an immersive experience.

c. Armando Records: Cutting-Edge Music Venue

Location: Calle 85 #14-46

- Highlights: Armando Records is synonymous with cutting-edge music and electronic beats. With live performances and a modern ambiance, it attracts a diverse crowd of music enthusiasts. The rooftop terrace provides stunning views of the city.

2. La Candelaria: Historic Charm and Cultural Richness

Location: La Candelaria Neighborhood

For those seeking a mix of history and nightlife, the historic La Candelaria neighborhood is the perfect choice. Cobblestone streets, colonial architecture, and an artistic vibe set the stage for unique entertainment experiences.

a. Quiebra Canto: Bohemian Vibes and Live Music

Location: Calle 12d #2-81

- Highlights: Quiebra Canto is a bohemian haven with live music performances ranging from jazz to salsa. The intimate setting, diverse crowd, and artistic décor create a unique ambiance.

b. El Goce Pagano: Traditional Colombian Folklore

Location: Carrera 2 #12-48

- Highlights: Immerse yourself in Colombian folklore at El Goce Pagano. This venue showcases traditional music, dance, and costumes, providing an authentic experience of the country's cultural heritage.

c. El Chorro de Quevedo: Iconic Gathering Spot

Location: Carrera 2 #13-59

- Highlights: El Chorro de Quevedo is a historic square where locals and visitors gather. Street performers, lively bars, and a convivial atmosphere make it an iconic spot to kick off the evening.

3. Usaquén: Quaint Markets and Artistic Vibes

Location: Usaquén Neighborhood

Usaquén, known for its quaint markets and artistic community, transforms into a charming nightlife destination in the evening. Explore the cobblestone streets lined with cafes, art galleries, and lively pubs.

a. Andres Carne de Res: Legendary Colombian Steakhouse and Club

Location: Calle 82 #12-21

- Highlights: Andres Carne de Res is a legendary steakhouse that evolves into a high-energy club. Known for its vibrant atmosphere, eclectic décor, and energetic dance floors, it's a nightlife institution in Bogotá.

b. Beer Station: Craft Beer and Laid-Back Vibes

Location: Calle 120a #6a-16

- Highlights: Beer Station offers a laid-back atmosphere with a wide selection of craft beers. The outdoor seating area is perfect for enjoying the cool Bogotá evenings while sipping on your favorite brew.

c. Bogotá Beer Company (BBC): Local Craft Beer Chain

Location: Various locations, including Calle 120a #6a-16

- Highlights: BBC, a popular local craft beer chain, has a presence in Usaquén. Enjoy a variety of artisanal beers in a relaxed setting, often accompanied by live music or DJ performances.

Bogotá's nightlife scene is as diverse as the city itself, offering everything from upscale clubs to bohemian live music venues. Whether you find yourself in the trendy Zona T, the historic La Candelaria, or the artistic Usaquén, each neighborhood has its unique charm and entertainment hotspots waiting to be explored.

Salsa, Cumbia, and More: Dancing Through the Night in Bogotá

Bogotá, a city pulsating with rhythm and energy, invites you to immerse yourself in its vibrant dance scene. From the sultry moves of salsa to the infectious beats of cumbia, the Colombian capital is a dance lover's paradise. Let's explore the various dance genres and venues that beckon you to sway, twirl, and dance through the night.

1. Salsa: Rhythm of the Streets:

Casa Quiebra Canto:

Location: Calle 12d #2-81, La Candelaria

- Highlights: Casa Quiebra Canto, situated in the historic La Candelaria neighborhood, is a haven for salsa enthusiasts. The intimate setting, live music, and dance floor create an authentic salsa experience. Beginners can join dance classes before hitting the floor.

Gozalos:

Location: Calle 70a #9-61

- Highlights: Gozalos is a popular salsa club where locals and visitors come together to dance to the rhythm of live bands and skilled DJs. The club's lively atmosphere and diverse crowd make it a favorite among salsa aficionados.

El Bembé:

Location: Carrera 5 #26b-50

- Highlights: El Bembé is a salsa institution in Bogotá, known for its energetic ambiance and live salsa performances. With a spacious dance floor and a mix of classic and contemporary salsa tracks, it's a place to lose yourself in the dance.

2. Cumbia: Traditional Colombian Rhythms:

La Puerta Grande:

Location: Calle 67 #6-55

- Highlights: La Puerta Grande introduces you to the infectious beats of cumbia. This venue often hosts live cumbia bands, creating an immersive experience in Colombian folklore. The vibrant décor and welcoming atmosphere add to the authenticity.

Andres Carne de Res:

Location: Calle 3 #11a-56, Zona Rosa

- Highlights: While primarily known for its lively atmosphere and diverse music selection, Andres Carne de

Res seamlessly integrates cumbia into its playlist. Dance enthusiasts can enjoy the blend of contemporary and traditional rhythms.

3. Reggaeton and Latin Beats:

Dopamina Club:

Location: Calle 85 #14-46, Zona T

- Highlights: Dopamina Club is a hot spot for reggaeton and Latin beats. The club's modern setting, vibrant lighting, and talented DJs create an electric atmosphere where you can dance to the latest hits in reggaeton, bachata, and more.

El Coq:

Location: Carrera 11 #84-09, Zona Rosa

- Highlights: El Coq is a trendy nightclub that seamlessly blends reggaeton, Latin pop, and electronic beats. With a stylish ambiance and a mix of local and international DJs, it's a favorite for those looking to dance to a diverse range of Latin rhythms.

4. Vallenato: Colombian Folkloric Vibes:

El Candelario:

Location: Calle 12d #3-46, La Candelaria

- Highlights: El Candelario, a beloved spot in La Candelaria, occasionally features live Vallenato bands. The fusion of accordion melodies and traditional beats provides a delightful introduction to this Colombian folk genre.

5. Dance Classes and Workshops:

Alma de Barrio:

Location: Carrera 17 #36-34

- Highlights: Alma de Barrio is not just a club but also a space for dance enthusiasts to refine their skills. Offering salsa and other Latin dance classes, it's a place to learn, practice, and then hit the dance floor with confidence.

Dancing through the night in Bogotá is an exhilarating journey into the heart of Colombian rhythms. Whether you're twirling to the beats of salsa, embracing the traditional moves of cumbia, or grooving to the latest reggaeton hits, the city's dance scene invites you to become part of the vibrant cultural tapestry that makes Bogotá truly unique. So, put on your dancing shoes and let the music guide you through a night of rhythm and joy.

Cultural Events Calendar: Festivals and Celebrations in Bogotá

Bogotá, the capital of Colombia, is a city that vibrates with cultural richness and a deep sense of tradition. Throughout the year, the city comes alive with festivals and celebrations that reflect the diverse heritage and artistic spirit of its people. Let's explore the cultural events calendar, highlighting some of the most significant festivals that define the cultural landscape of Bogotá.

1. Festival Iberoamericano de Teatro:

When: Biennial, usually in March/April

- Overview: The Ibero-American Theater Festival is one of the largest and most renowned theater festivals in the world. Held every two years, the event transforms the city into a stage for performances ranging from traditional plays to experimental theater. International theater troupes and local artists come together, making it a celebration of the performing arts.

2. Festival de Verano:

When: August

- Overview: The Festival de Verano, or Summer Festival, is a month-long celebration that encompasses a wide range of events, from music concerts to sports competitions. It culminates in the iconic "Desfile de Silleteros," a vibrant parade where locals carry intricate flower arrangements on their backs, showcasing the region's floral artistry.

3. Rock al Parque:

When: July

- Overview: South America's largest free rock music festival, Rock al Parque, takes place annually in Bogotá. Over the course of three days, local and international rock bands perform in Simón Bolívar Park, attracting music enthusiasts from all walks of life. The festival promotes cultural diversity and a love for rock music.

4. Fiesta de la Candelaria:

When: February

- Overview: The Fiesta de la Candelaria is a colorful celebration that merges traditional Colombian folklore with Catholic traditions. Parades, dance performances, and vibrant costumes characterize the festivities. The event showcases the diversity of Colombian culture, particularly in the historic La Candelaria neighborhood.

5. Bogotá International Film Festival:

When: October

- Overview: This film festival brings together filmmakers, directors, and cinephiles from around the world. Screenings of international and Colombian films, along with discussions and workshops, contribute to the city's vibrant cinematic culture. The festival aims to promote dialogue and appreciation for diverse storytelling through the medium of film.

6. BAM - Bogotá Audiovisual Market:

When: July

- Overview: BAM is an essential event for the audiovisual industry. It includes film screenings, conferences, and networking opportunities, bringing together professionals in the field. The market focuses on promoting Colombian and Latin American audiovisual content on the international stage.

7. Independence Day Celebrations:

When: July 20

- Overview: Colombia celebrates its Independence Day on July 20, marking the beginning of the struggle for independence from Spanish rule. Bogotá hosts a grand parade, military demonstrations, cultural events, and fireworks to commemorate this significant moment in history.

8. Ciclovía Nocturna:

When: Various dates throughout the year

- Overview: While not a traditional festival, Ciclovía Nocturna is a recurring event that transforms Bogotá's streets into a recreational space. On designated nights, major roads are closed to vehicular traffic, allowing cyclists, pedestrians, and skaters to enjoy the city's landmarks under the evening sky.

Bogotá's cultural events calendar is a testament to the city's dynamism and commitment to preserving and celebrating its heritage. From world-class theater festivals to lively music celebrations and film showcases, these events provide both locals and visitors with a rich tapestry of cultural experiences throughout the year. As you explore Bogotá, consider aligning your visit with one of these festivals to immerse yourself in the city's vibrant cultural scene.

Chapter 9

Cultural Immersion

Museums and Art Galleries

Bogotá's cultural landscape is a vibrant tapestry woven with the threads of history, artistic expression, and contemporary creativity. Step into the city's cultural heart by exploring its diverse museums and art galleries, each offering a unique lens into Colombia's multifaceted identity.

Museums: Gateway to Colombia's Past and Present

Bogotá's museums are treasure troves that unlock the secrets of Colombia's history, heritage, and artistic evolution. Each institution is a carefully curated repository that invites visitors to delve deeper into the nation's narrative.

Gold Museum (Museo del Oro)

- Nestled in La Candelaria, the Gold Museum stands as a testament to the artistry and spirituality of Colombia's pre-Columbian cultures. Home to over 55,000 pieces of gold and other materials, the museum's exhibits showcase the skillful craftsmanship of indigenous civilizations. Highlights include intricate golden artifacts, ceremonial objects, and jewelry, each telling a story of ancient rituals and beliefs. The immersive displays and multimedia presentations make this museum a must-visit for those seeking to connect with Colombia's rich pre-Hispanic heritage.

National Museum (Museo Nacional de Colombia)

- Housed in a neoclassical architectural gem, the National Museum invites visitors on a chronological journey through Colombia's past. From prehistoric times to the present day, the museum's halls feature artifacts, art, and historical documents that narrate the nation's story. Highlights include the Independence Room, showcasing relics from Colombia's fight for freedom, and the Anthropology Room, which unveils the diversity of indigenous cultures. Temporary exhibitions ensure that there's always something new to discover.

Bogotá Museum of Modern Art (Museo de Arte Moderno de Bogotá - MAMBO)

- Situated in the heart of the city, MAMBO is a dynamic space that celebrates Colombian and Latin American contemporary art. The museum's collection encompasses paintings, sculptures, and installations, providing a platform for both established and emerging artists. The ever-changing exhibits explore themes of identity, social issues, and artistic experimentation. MAMBO is not just a gallery; it's a vibrant dialogue between the past, present, and future of Colombian art.

Quinta de Bolívar

- Quinta de Bolívar, a historic house museum, invites visitors into the residence of Simón Bolívar, the liberator of Latin America. Preserved to reflect its 19th-century grandeur, the museum offers a glimpse into Bolívar's daily life and the political landscape of the era. Walk through the charming gardens, explore the rooms filled with period furniture, and gain insights into the personal and political life of one of South America's most iconic figures.

Art Galleries: Exploring Bogotá's Contemporary Scene

Bogotá's art galleries are dynamic spaces that bridge the gap between tradition and avant-garde, showcasing the city's vibrant contemporary art scene.

NC-arte Gallery

- Located in Usaquén, NC-arte Gallery is a hub for experimental and avant-garde art. The gallery's exhibitions push the boundaries of artistic expression, featuring works that challenge conventional norms and invite contemplation. From thought-provoking installations to immersive performances, NC-arte fosters a space for artistic experimentation and cultural dialogue. The gallery's commitment to pushing the boundaries of artistic expression makes it a cornerstone of Bogotá's contemporary art scene.

La Macarena Street Art

- La Macarena, an artistic neighborhood, transforms the streets into an open-air gallery. Vibrant street art adorns buildings, reflecting Bogotá's urban culture. The walls tell stories of social issues, cultural diversity, and the city's dynamic spirit. A stroll through La Macarena is a journey into the pulse of Bogotá's contemporary art scene, where local and international street artists use the city's walls as canvases to convey powerful messages and creative expressions.

Gallery Districts: Chapinero and La Candelaria

Chapinero and La Candelaria are bustling districts with numerous art galleries, each contributing to Bogotá's diverse artistic tapestry.

- In Chapinero, explore spaces like Flora Ars+Natura, a gallery known for its focus on contemporary art and ecology. The exhibits here often engage with environmental themes, creating a dialogue between art and nature.
- In La Candelaria, galleries like Alonso Garcés Galería offer a blend of traditional and modern Colombian art. The cobblestone streets of La Candelaria add a unique charm to the gallery-hopping experience, making it a cultural adventure within the historical heart of the city.

These gallery districts serve as vibrant hubs where artists and art lovers converge, creating a dynamic and inclusive atmosphere that reflects the diversity of Bogotá's artistic community.

To make the most of your cultural journey, check the schedules of these museums and galleries for special exhibitions, events, and guided tours. Whether you're a history buff, an art enthusiast, or simply curious about Bogotá's cultural identity, these institutions offer a gateway to a deeper understanding of the city's past and present.

Bogotá's Historical Landmarks

Bogotá's cityscape is a living testament to Colombia's rich history, marked by colonial influences, moments of revolution, and the evolution of a vibrant culture. Explore the historical landmarks that dot the city, each narrating a unique chapter in Bogotá's past.

Plaza de Bolívar: Heart of the City

- Plaza de Bolívar, surrounded by architectural masterpieces, is the pulsating heart of Bogotá. At the center of the square stands the equestrian statue of Simón Bolívar, the liberator of Latin America. Encircled by key buildings such as the Cathedral of Bogotá, the National Capitol, and the Palace of Justice, Plaza de Bolívar is not just a central point but a symbolic representation of Colombia's political, religious, and judicial history. The square has witnessed countless events, from political rallies to cultural celebrations, making it a living canvas of the city's evolution.

La Catedral Primada: Architectural Marvel

- Dominating the eastern side of Plaza de Bolívar, La Catedral Primada is a majestic cathedral that stands as an architectural jewel. Built over several centuries, this neoclassical cathedral boasts intricate carvings, soaring spires, and a serene interior adorned with religious art. The cathedral not only serves as a place of worship but also as a repository of historical events, having witnessed the city's growth from its early days.

Casa de Nariño: Presidential Residence

- Casa de Nariño, situated near Plaza de Bolívar, is the official residence of the President of Colombia. Beyond its role as a modern seat of government, the building has a storied past. It was witness to the signing of Colombia's first constitution in 1830 and has since played a crucial role in the nation's political history. Guided tours offer a glimpse into the halls where pivotal decisions have been made, and visitors can witness the Changing of the Guard ceremony, a ceremonial tradition that echoes the city's historical continuity.

Monserrate: Sacred Summit

- Ascending to the summit of Monserrate is not just a physical journey; it's a spiritual and historical one. Whether you opt for the funicular, cable car, or the more adventurous hike, reaching the top rewards you with panoramic views of Bogotá. The Santuario de Monserrate, a 17th-century church, welcomes visitors to a place of pilgrimage. Beyond its religious significance, the mountain itself holds cultural importance, representing a fusion of indigenous beliefs with Catholic traditions.

Teatro Colón: Architectural Gem

- Teatro Colón, inaugurated in 1892, is a national monument that stands as a testament to Bogotá's commitment to the arts. The theater's neoclassical façade opens into an opulent interior adorned with gilded detailing and intricate frescoes. Attending a performance here not only allows you to appreciate the historical and architectural significance of the venue but also connects you to the city's cultural heartbeat.

Embark on a historical journey through Bogotá's landmarks, and let each site unfold stories of resilience, transformation, and the enduring spirit of a city that has weathered the winds of time.

Bogotá Festivals and Events Calendar

Bogotá's calendar is punctuated with lively festivals and events, offering visitors a unique opportunity to witness the city's vibrant culture, diverse traditions, and dynamic artistic scene. From colorful parades to music festivals, each event contributes to the tapestry of Bogotá's identity. Plan your visit to coincide with one of these festivities for an unforgettable experience.

1. Bogotá International Film Festival (BIFF)

Date: Varies (Typically in October)

- Overview: BIFF showcases a diverse selection of local and international films, attracting filmmakers, cinephiles, and industry professionals. Screenings, discussions, and workshops take place across the city, offering a cinematic immersion into Bogotá's cultural landscape.

2. Ibero-American Theater Festival

Date: Biennial (Odd-numbered years, typically in April)

- Overview: Recognized as one of the world's most significant theater festivals, this event transforms Bogotá into a stage for a multitude of performances. The city comes alive with street theater, dance, and experimental performances, attracting artists and spectators from around the globe.

3. Bogotá Carnival

Date: August 6

- Overview: Celebrating Bogotá's founding day, the carnival features colorful parades, traditional music, and dance. Locals and visitors alike don vibrant costumes, creating a lively atmosphere throughout the city. The carnival provides a glimpse into Colombia's rich cultural heritage.

4. Rock al Parque

Date: Varies (Typically in July)

- Overview: Latin America's largest free rock music festival, Rock al Parque gathers local and international bands for a weekend of live performances in Simon Bolivar Park. From punk to metal, the festival caters to diverse musical tastes, drawing music enthusiasts from all over.

5. Bogotá International Book Fair

Date: Varies (Typically in April)

- Overview: Book lovers unite at the International Book Fair, where authors, publishers, and literary enthusiasts converge. The event features book signings, panel discussions, and cultural activities, making it a literary haven in the heart of Bogotá.

6. Colombiamoda

Date: Varies (Typically in July)

- Overview: As one of Latin America's premier fashion events, Colombiamoda showcases the latest trends in Colombian and international fashion. Runway shows, exhibitions, and industry conferences create a vibrant atmosphere for fashion aficionados and industry professionals.

7. Festival de Verano (Summer Festival)

Date: August

- Overview: Bogotá's Summer Festival offers a diverse program of events, including concerts, sports competitions, and cultural activities. The festival celebrates the city's diversity and invites residents and visitors to engage in a variety of summertime experiences.

8. Fiestas de las Luces (Festival of Lights)

Date: December

- Overview: The Christmas season in Bogotá is illuminated by the Festival of Lights, a dazzling display of decorations and artistic light installations throughout the city. Parades, concerts, and cultural events add to the festive atmosphere, making it a magical time to visit.

9. Independence Day Celebrations

Date: July 20

- Overview: Colombia's Independence Day is marked by patriotic celebrations across Bogotá. Parades, concerts, and fireworks contribute to the festive ambiance as locals come together to commemorate the nation's history.

10. Bogotá Wine and Food Festival

Date: Varies (Typically in September)

- Overview: Epicureans rejoice during the Wine and Food Festival, where culinary enthusiasts can indulge in tastings, workshops, and gourmet experiences. Renowned chefs showcase their skills, making this event a gastronomic delight.

Note: Dates for events may vary each year, and it's advisable to check the official event websites or local sources for the most up-to-date information.

Tips for Enjoying Festivals in Bogotá:

- Plan Ahead: Check the festival dates and plan your visit accordingly.
- Explore Neighborhoods: Festivals often take place in various neighborhoods, providing an opportunity to explore different parts of the city.
- Embrace Local Customs: Participate in the festivities, interact with locals, and embrace the unique cultural traditions of each event.
- Book Accommodations Early: As festivals attract visitors, it's advisable to book accommodations in advance.

Immerse yourself in the rhythm of Bogotá's festivals, where the city's energy and creativity come to life, offering a vibrant and authentic Colombian experience.

Chapter 10

Culinary Delights

Traditional Colombian Cuisine

Embark on a gastronomic journey through the diverse and flavorful landscape of traditional Colombian cuisine. From the hearty dishes of the Andean highlands to the coastal delights influenced by Afro-Colombian and indigenous flavors, Colombian food is a celebration of cultural diversity and culinary creativity.

Ajiaco Santafereño

- Ajiaco Santafereño is a soul-warming soup that hails from the Andean region, particularly Bogotá. This hearty dish features chicken, three types of potatoes (papas criollas, sabaneras, and pastusas), corn on the cob, capers, and a variety of herbs. What makes Ajiaco unique is the inclusion of the herb guascas, which imparts a distinct earthy flavor. Served with a side of rice, avocado, and a dollop of cream, Ajiaco is a comforting and flavorful Colombian classic.

Bandeja Paisa

- A true representation of Colombian indulgence, Bandeja Paisa is a feast on a plate. Originating from the Paisa region, this dish is a hearty combination of rice, red beans, ground meat (usually beef or pork), chorizo, morcilla (blood sausage), chicharrón (fried pork belly), avocado, fried egg, and plantains. It's a robust and flavorful ensemble that showcases the agricultural richness of the Colombian highlands.

Sancocho

- Sancocho is a beloved Colombian soup that varies across regions, each with its unique twist. Common ingredients include a mix of meats such as chicken, beef, or fish, root vegetables like yams and plantains, corn on the cob, and a medley of herbs and spices. The result is a hearty and nourishing soup, often enjoyed as a communal dish during family gatherings and celebrations.

Arepas

- Arepas are a staple in Colombian cuisine, unleashing a world of possibilities in terms of shapes, sizes, and fillings. These corn-based flatbreads can be grilled, baked, or fried and are often stuffed with cheese, eggs, ham, or avocado. Arepas accompany meals throughout the day and serve as a versatile canvas for both savory and sweet toppings.

Empanadas

- Colombian empanadas are a delicious hand-held treat enjoyed across the country. These deep-fried or baked pastries are typically filled with a mixture of seasoned meat (beef, chicken, or pork), potatoes, and sometimes rice. Served with aji sauce or hogao (tomato and onion sauce), Colombian empanadas are a popular snack or appetizer, perfect for any occasion.

Lechona

- Lechona is a festive dish often reserved for special occasions. This culinary masterpiece involves a whole pig stuffed with a mixture of rice, peas, and spices. The pig is slow-roasted until the skin becomes crispy and golden, creating a delightful contrast with the tender and flavorful filling. Lechona is a celebration of communal feasting and is particularly popular during holidays and events.

Posta Negra

- Posta Negra is a slow-cooked beef dish with a deep, rich flavor profile. The meat is marinated in a mixture of panela (unrefined whole cane sugar), soy sauce, and spices, then slow-cooked until tender. Served with rice, potatoes, and a side of salad, Posta Negra showcases the fusion of indigenous, African, and Spanish influences in Colombian cuisine.

Changua

- Changua is a traditional Colombian breakfast soup that originates from the Andean region. It consists of a milky broth flavored with green onions and cilantro, with poached eggs added just before serving. This simple yet nourishing dish is often accompanied by arepas or bread and is believed to have originated from the Muisca indigenous people.

Highlights of Traditional Colombian Cuisine:

- Diversity in Ingredients: Colombian cuisine reflects the country's ecological diversity with its use of a wide array of ingredients, including tropical fruits, tubers, and a variety of meats.
- Regional Influences: Each region of Colombia contributes its unique flavors to the country's culinary mosaic, resulting in a diverse and vibrant gastronomic landscape.

- Communal Dining: Colombian meals are often a communal affair, emphasizing the importance of shared experiences and the joy of coming together over a table filled with delectable dishes.
- Cultural Fusion: The cuisine reflects the country's history of cultural fusion, blending indigenous, African, and Spanish culinary traditions into a harmonious and delicious tapestry.

Traditional Colombian cuisine is a celebration of cultural diversity, a testament to the country's rich history, and an invitation to savor the flavors that have been passed down through generations.

Casual Eateries in Bogotá: A Culinary Expedition

Bogotá's casual eateries are the heartbeat of the city, offering a diverse array of flavors in a relaxed and vibrant atmosphere. From bustling markets to charming cafes, here are some top recommendations for casual dining experiences, each providing a unique taste of Bogotá's culinary scene.

Andrés Carne de Res (Chía)

Location: Calle 3 # 11A-56, Chía, Cundinamarca

- Andrés Carne de Res is not just a restaurant; it's a cultural institution and a carnivorous paradise. Located in the nearby town of Chía, this lively establishment is known for its vibrant atmosphere, eclectic decor, and, of course, mouthwatering Colombian grill. Feast on an array of grilled meats, hearty sides, and refreshing beverages while enjoying live music and the energetic ambiance. The experience at Andrés Carne de Res is as much about the lively atmosphere as it is about the delectable food.

La Puerta Falsa

Location: Calle 11 # 6-50, Bogotá

- Nestled in the historic La Candelaria district, La Puerta Falsa is a charming eatery that has been delighting locals and visitors alike since 1816. Known for its traditional Colombian comfort food, the menu features classics like Ajiaco, tamales, and hot chocolate with cheese. The rustic ambiance and the sense of stepping back in time make La Puerta Falsa a perfect spot for a cozy and authentic Colombian dining experience.

El Panóptico

Location: Carrera 5 # 26B-85, Bogotá

- For a unique dining experience in Bogotá, head to El Panóptico, a restaurant located in a former prison. The historic setting, combined with modern culinary flair, creates a distinctive atmosphere. Enjoy a menu that blends Colombian and international flavors, with dishes ranging from grilled meats to pasta. The panoramic views from the terrace add to the allure of dining in this unconventional space.

Mercado de la Perseverancia

Location: Carrera 5 # 26D-12, Bogotá

- Embrace the spirit of Bogotá at Mercado de la Perseverancia, a bustling market that showcases the city's culinary diversity. This vibrant marketplace is a treasure trove of local ingredients, street food stalls, and small eateries serving up Colombian delights. From fresh fruits to empanadas and regional specialties, Mercado de la Perseverancia is a must-visit for those seeking an authentic taste of Bogotá's street food scene.

El Kilo

Location: Carrera 13 # 85-79, Bogotá

- El Kilo offers a laid-back and trendy setting for those looking to enjoy a variety of dishes in a casual atmosphere. The restaurant's concept revolves around the "pay by weight" system, allowing diners to choose from an extensive buffet of salads, hot dishes, and desserts. The eclectic menu caters to diverse tastes, making El Kilo a popular spot for a casual and customizable dining experience.

Café de la Fonda

Location: Carrera 5 # 18B-48, Bogotá

- Step into the heart of La Candelaria and discover the charm of Café de la Fonda. This quaint cafe exudes a cozy and artistic vibe, making it an ideal spot for a leisurely coffee or a light meal. The menu features Colombian coffee specialties, freshly baked pastries, and light bites. The relaxed atmosphere and friendly service make Café de la Fonda a delightful oasis in the midst of the historic district.

Abasto Restaurante

Location: Calle 119B # 5-60, Bogotá

- Abasto Restaurante is a hidden gem in Bogotá, offering a farm-to-table dining experience in a stylish and modern setting. The menu emphasizes locally sourced ingredients, with dishes that celebrate Colombian flavors with a contemporary twist. From gourmet burgers to inventive salads, Abasto is a casual yet sophisticated option for those seeking a taste of Bogotá's evolving culinary scene.

Highlights of Casual Eateries:

- Diverse Culinary Offerings: Bogotá's casual eateries showcase the city's culinary diversity, from traditional Colombian comfort food to innovative and international-inspired dishes.
- Historic Charm: Many casual eateries are situated in historic districts, providing not just delicious meals but also a glimpse into the city's rich history and cultural heritage.
- Vibrant Atmosphere: The casual dining scene in Bogotá is characterized by lively atmospheres, whether it's the energetic vibe of Andrés Carne de Res or the cozy charm of Café de la Fonda.
- Innovative Concepts: Restaurants like El Kilo and El Panóptico bring innovative concepts to the table, offering diners unique and memorable experiences beyond just the culinary delights.

Bogotá's casual eateries are a testament to the city's culinary dynamism, blending tradition with innovation and creating spaces where locals and visitors can savor the essence of Colombian cuisine in a relaxed and inviting setting.

Fine Dining in Bogotá

Bogotá's fine dining scene is a showcase of culinary artistry, where innovative chefs blend traditional Colombian ingredients with international techniques to create unforgettable dining experiences. Here are some top recommendations for fine dining establishments in Bogotá, each offering a gastronomic journey that reflects the city's culinary excellence.

Leo Cocina y Cava

Location: Calle 27B # 6-75, Bogotá

- Leo Cocina y Cava, led by renowned chef Leonor Espinosa, is a culinary gem in Bogotá. The restaurant is celebrated for its innovative approach to Colombian cuisine, incorporating traditional ingredients from diverse regions. The tasting menu is a journey through the country's flavors, with each dish thoughtfully crafted to tell a story. The elegant setting, attentive service, and a carefully curated wine list contribute to an exquisite fine dining experience.

Criterion

Location: Calle 69A # 5-75, Bogotá

- Criterion, helmed by chef Jorge Rausch, is a culinary institution in Bogotá. The restaurant is renowned for its commitment to using high-quality, seasonal ingredients to create dishes that marry Colombian flavors with international influences. The menu evolves with the seasons, ensuring that each visit is a unique and memorable experience. The sophisticated ambiance and impeccable service make Criterion a top choice for those seeking a refined dining experience.

Árdila Lulle

Location: Carrera 9 # 75-70, Bogotá

- Árdila Lulle is a fine dining restaurant that combines contemporary culinary techniques with a dedication to showcasing Colombia's rich gastronomic heritage. Chef Alejandro Gutiérrez's creations are a testament to precision and creativity, with dishes that highlight local ingredients in unexpected ways. The restaurant's stylish setting and attention to detail make Árdila Lulle a destination for those seeking modern Colombian cuisine at its finest.

El Cielo

Location: Carrera 11A # 90-30, Bogotá

- El Cielo, with its avant-garde approach to gastronomy, offers a multisensory dining experience that pushes the boundaries of culinary creativity. Chef Juan Manuel Barrientos crafts dishes that engage not only the palate but also sight, smell, and touch. The tasting menu, named "Moments," takes diners on a journey through a series of carefully curated dishes, each telling a unique story. El Cielo is a haven for those who appreciate culinary innovation and a truly immersive dining experience.

Casa San Isidro

Location: Carrera 2 # 12B-21, Bogotá

- Casa San Isidro, nestled in the historic La Candelaria district, is a fine dining establishment housed in a beautifully restored colonial mansion. Chef Diego Vega's menu showcases a blend of Colombian and international flavors, with a focus on locally sourced ingredients. The intimate setting, complete with antique furnishings and a charming courtyard, creates an atmosphere of timeless elegance. Casa San Isidro is a captivating destination for those seeking a refined dining experience with a touch of history.

Criterion La Vitrola

Location: Calle 69A # 5-75, Bogotá

- Criterion La Vitrola is an extension of the acclaimed Criterion restaurant, offering a more casual yet equally sophisticated dining experience. The menu features a selection of dishes that highlight the best of Colombian and international cuisine. The stylish decor and warm ambiance make Criterion La Vitrola an ideal choice for those seeking a relaxed but refined atmosphere.

Highlights of Fine Dining Establishments:

- Innovative Culinary Techniques: Fine dining establishments in Bogotá are known for their innovative approach to culinary techniques, pushing the boundaries of flavor and presentation.
- Celebration of Colombian Ingredients: Chefs at these establishments often celebrate Colombia's diverse culinary landscape by incorporating locally sourced and traditional ingredients into their creations.
- Unique Tasting Experiences: Many fine dining restaurants offer tasting menus that take diners on a curated journey, allowing them to experience a variety of flavors and textures in a single sitting.
- Elegant Atmosphere: The ambiance at these establishments is carefully curated to provide an elegant and immersive dining experience, often set in stylish surroundings that complement the culinary artistry.

Bogotá's fine dining establishments are a testament to the city's culinary sophistication, offering a blend of innovation, tradition, and artistry that makes each dining experience a journey into the heart of Colombian gastronomy.

Chapter 11

Shopping Spree

Bogotá's Shopping Extravaganza: Local Markets

Bogotá's local markets are vibrant hubs of activity, showcasing the city's diverse cultural heritage and providing an immersive shopping experience. From traditional crafts to culinary delights, these markets offer a treasure trove of unique finds. Embark on a shopping spree through Bogotá's local markets and discover the rich tapestry of Colombian craftsmanship and flavors.

Usaquén Flea Market

Location: Carrera 6A # 118-03, Bogotá

- Usaquén Flea Market, located in the charming Usaquén neighborhood, is a bustling market that comes to life every Sunday. Stroll through the cobblestone streets lined with artisanal stalls and vendors selling a variety of goods, including handmade crafts, jewelry, clothing, and traditional Colombian snacks. The market's festive atmosphere, live music, and diverse offerings make it a favorite among locals and visitors alike.

Paloquemao Market

Location: Carrera 19 # 25-04, Bogotá

- Paloquemao Market is Bogotá's largest and most famous food market, a kaleidoscope of colors, aromas, and flavors. Explore the market's bustling aisles to discover an array of fresh produce, exotic fruits, flowers, and local delicacies.

Engage with the vendors, sample tropical fruits, and witness the lively energy of this authentic Colombian market. Paloquemao is a paradise for food enthusiasts and those looking to experience the heart of Bogotá's culinary scene.

San Alejo Market

Location: Calle 27 # 4A-55, Bogotá

- San Alejo Market, held on the first Sunday of every month, is a vintage and antique market that transforms the historic La Candelaria neighborhood. Antique collectors and bargain hunters alike flock to this market to explore an eclectic mix of items, including retro furniture, vinyl records, vintage clothing, and unique trinkets. The market adds a nostalgic touch to the cobblestone streets of La Candelaria.

Mercado de las Pulgas de la 93

Location: Calle 93 # 11-24, Bogotá

- Mercado de las Pulgas de la 93, also known as the Flea Market of 93, is a popular spot for vintage and second-hand finds. Held on weekends, this market features a variety of stalls selling pre-loved clothing, accessories, and collectibles. The lively ambiance, combined with the chance to unearth hidden gems, makes it a favorite among those with a penchant for vintage fashion and unique treasures.

Santafé Shopping Mall Artisan Market

Location: Calle 185 # 45-03, Bogotá

- Santafé Shopping Mall Artisan Market brings the charm of a traditional market to the modern setting of a shopping mall. Here, you'll find a curated selection of handmade crafts, textiles, and artisanal products, providing a unique shopping experience within the Santafé Shopping Mall. It's an ideal destination for those looking to combine retail therapy with the convenience of a shopping center.

Plaza de Mercado de La Perseverancia

Location: Carrera 5 # 30A-20, Bogotá

- Plaza de Mercado de La Perseverancia is a historic market that showcases the agricultural richness of Colombia. This market, in operation since the late 19th century, is known for its fresh produce, local cheeses, and regional specialties. Navigate through the market's labyrinthine corridors, interact with the friendly vendors, and savor the authentic flavors of Colombian cuisine.

Highlights of Local Markets:

- Handmade Crafts and Artisanal Goods: Usaquén Flea Market and Santafé Shopping Mall Artisan Market are treasure troves for handmade crafts, jewelry, and unique artisanal products.
- Culinary Exploration: Paloquemao Market and Plaza de Mercado de La Perseverancia offer a culinary journey, featuring fresh produce, local delicacies, and the vibrant energy of authentic Colombian markets.
- Vintage and Antique Finds: San Alejo Market and Mercado de las Pulgas de la 93 cater to vintage enthusiasts, offering a delightful array of retro items, collectibles, and second-hand treasures.

- Cultural Immersion: Exploring local markets provides an immersive experience, allowing visitors to engage with Colombian vendors, learn about traditional crafts, and taste local flavors.
- Variety Within Shopping Malls: Santafé Shopping Mall Artisan Market showcases how traditional markets can seamlessly integrate into modern shopping centers, offering a diverse shopping experience.

Bogotá's local markets invite you to indulge in a shopping spree where each stall tells a story of Colombian craftsmanship, culinary traditions, and cultural heritage. Whether you're searching for unique souvenirs, vintage gems, or a culinary adventure, these markets promise a memorable and authentic shopping experience.

Boutique Shopping Districts

Bogotá boasts a collection of boutique shopping districts that cater to those seeking upscale and unique retail experiences. From high-end fashion to exclusive local designs, these districts offer a curated selection of shops in stylish surroundings. Embark on a sophisticated shopping spree through Bogotá's boutique districts and discover the city's flair for fashion and luxury.

Zona T (Zona Rosa)

Location: Carrera 13 # 85-46, Bogotá

- Zona T, also known as Zona Rosa, is Bogotá's premier boutique shopping and entertainment district. Lined with high-end fashion boutiques, luxury brands, and chic designer stores, Zona T is a haven for fashion enthusiasts. The district comes alive in the evenings, with trendy bars, gourmet restaurants, and vibrant nightlife options. Whether you're looking for international designer labels or local haute couture, Zona T is a glamorous destination for indulgent retail therapy.

Usaquén

Location: Usaquén neighborhood, Bogotá

- Usaquén, an enchanting colonial neighborhood, is home to a charming blend of boutiques, galleries, and artisanal shops. The cobblestone streets and historic architecture create a picturesque backdrop for boutique shopping. Explore the boutiques that showcase a mix of high-end fashion, bohemian chic, and unique artisanal products. Usaquén's boutique scene caters to those seeking one-of-a-kind items and a laid-back shopping experience.

Chapinero Alto

Location: Chapinero Alto neighborhood, Bogotá

- Chapinero Alto, known for its trendy atmosphere, is emerging as a boutique shopping destination. The district offers a mix of independent boutiques, concept stores, and art galleries. From avant-garde fashion to contemporary art pieces, Chapinero Alto attracts those with an appreciation for cutting-edge design and local creativity. The district's diverse and edgy character sets it apart as a destination for the fashion-forward and art-savvy.

Centro Andino

Location: Carrera 11 # 82-71, Bogotá

- Centro Andino, situated in the heart of the city, is a luxury shopping center that houses an array of high-end boutiques and designer stores. From renowned international brands to upscale Colombian designers, Centro Andino offers a curated selection of fashion, accessories, and lifestyle products. The center's sophisticated ambiance and elegant surroundings make it a refined destination for boutique shopping in Bogotá.

El Retiro Shopping Center

Location: Calle 81 # 11-75, Bogotá

- El Retiro Shopping Center, adjacent to Zona T, is a boutique shopping center that combines upscale retail with a luxurious ambiance. The center features a collection of boutique stores, offering a mix of fashion, jewelry, and lifestyle products. El Retiro's stylish architecture, outdoor spaces, and exclusive brands make it a sought-after destination for those seeking a sophisticated and leisurely shopping experience.

Hacienda Santa Bárbara

Location: Carrera 7 # 115-60, Bogotá

- Hacienda Santa Bárbara, nestled in the northern part of the city, is a historical shopping complex that blends colonial charm with boutique elegance. The district features a mix of boutique shops, artisanal markets, and gourmet dining options. Explore the boutiques housed in colonial-style buildings, offering a curated selection of fashion, accessories, and unique finds. Hacienda Santa Bárbara provides a serene and upscale atmosphere for boutique shopping enthusiasts.

Highlights of Boutique Shopping Districts:

- Fashion-forward Destinations: Zona T and Chapinero Alto cater to those seeking the latest trends, high-end fashion, and avant-garde designs.
- Colonial Charm: Usaquén and Hacienda Santa Bárbara provide a unique shopping experience in historic surroundings, with cobblestone streets and colonial architecture adding a touch of charm.
- Luxury Retail Centers: Centro Andino and El Retiro Shopping Center offer a luxurious and curated selection of international and local designer brands in an upscale shopping environment.
- Artistic and Conceptual Boutiques: Chapinero Alto stands out for its artistic and conceptual boutiques, showcasing the work of local designers and creatives.
- Leisurely Shopping Atmosphere: The boutique districts, each with its distinctive character, provide a leisurely atmosphere for a more relaxed and enjoyable shopping experience.

Bogotá's boutique shopping districts invite you to explore a world of fashion, design, and luxury. Whether you're drawn to the trendy vibes of Zona T or the artistic flair of Chapinero Alto, each district offers a unique blend of style and sophistication for a memorable shopping spree.

Souvenirs and Unique Finds

Immerse yourself in Bogotá's diverse shopping scene and uncover a world of souvenirs and unique finds that reflect the city's rich culture and creativity. From traditional crafts to contemporary gems, these shopping destinations offer an array of distinctive mementos that capture the spirit of Bogotá. Embark on a memorable shopping spree and bring home treasures that tell the story of your Colombian adventure.

La Candelaria Artisan Market

Location: Carrera 3 # 12C-90, Bogotá

- La Candelaria, Bogotá's historic district, hosts an artisan market where you can discover a treasure trove of Colombian handicrafts. Explore the narrow streets adorned with colorful stalls offering handmade textiles, traditional ceramics, vibrant paintings, and unique jewelry. La Candelaria Artisan Market is a perfect destination for those seeking authentic Colombian souvenirs and gifts with a touch of local charm.

Highlights:

- Textiles and Fabrics: Delve into the rich textile traditions of Colombia with vibrant, handwoven fabrics that showcase indigenous patterns and techniques.
- Ceramics and Pottery: Discover intricately crafted ceramics and pottery, reflecting the diverse regional styles and artistic expressions found throughout Colombia.
- Jewelry: From beaded necklaces to intricate silverwork, the market offers a stunning array of jewelry, often inspired by indigenous designs.
- Paintings and Artwork: Bring home a piece of Colombian art with paintings depicting the country's landscapes, traditions, and vibrant cultural scenes.

Plaza de Bolívar

Location: La Candelaria, Bogotá

- Plaza de Bolívar, the heart of Bogotá, is not only a historic and cultural hub but also a vibrant marketplace. Local vendors set up stalls around the square, offering an assortment of souvenirs, from traditional crafts to indigenous artwork. Take a leisurely stroll around the plaza, and you'll find everything from handwoven textiles to intricately crafted leather goods.

Highlights:

- Leather Goods: Explore stalls offering high-quality leather goods such as bags, wallets, and accessories, often crafted by skilled artisans.
- Indigenous Artwork: Encounter traditional indigenous art, including paintings, sculptures, and hand-carved wooden pieces that reflect Colombia's diverse cultural heritage.
- Coffee-related Souvenirs: As Colombia is renowned for its coffee, find unique coffee-related souvenirs such as ceramic mugs, bags of locally sourced coffee, and artisanal coffee accessories.

Mercado de las Pulgas San Alejo

Location: Carrera 7 # 24-45, Bogotá

- Mercado de las Pulgas San Alejo, held on Sundays, is a fascinating flea market where you can uncover vintage treasures and unique collectibles. Browse through stalls featuring antique books, retro clothing, vinyl records, and quirky knick-knacks. Whether you're a collector or simply seeking something distinctive, this market in the Chapinero neighborhood is a haven for those who appreciate the charm of bygone eras.

Highlights:

- Vintage Clothing: Dive into a curated collection of vintage clothing, spanning various eras and styles, offering a fashionable trip through time.
- Retro Records: Vinyl enthusiasts can sift through crates of records, discovering classic Colombian and international music from decades past.
- Antique Books and Maps: Bookworms will appreciate the selection of antique books, maps, and prints, providing a glimpse into Colombia's literary and historical heritage.

Monserrate Souvenir Shops

Location: Cerro de Monserrate, Bogotá

- The summit of Cerro de Monserrate not only offers breathtaking views of Bogotá but also houses souvenir shops where you can find distinctive mementos. From religious artifacts to locally crafted jewelry, these shops offer a unique selection of items that reflect the cultural and spiritual significance of Monserrate. The journey to the top becomes a delightful shopping experience.

Highlights:

- Religious Artifacts: Explore a collection of religious icons, statues, and artifacts that showcase Colombia's deep Catholic heritage.
- Handcrafted Jewelry: Discover locally made jewelry inspired by Colombian themes, often featuring semiprecious stones and indigenous designs.

- Artisanal Gifts: Pick up small, handcrafted gifts such as candles, textiles, and ceramics, each representing the spiritual essence of Monserrate.

Andino Commercial Center Craft Market

Location: Carrera 11 # 82-71, Bogotá

- Andino Commercial Center, in addition to its luxury boutiques, features a craft market where you can discover handmade Colombian treasures. This market offers a curated selection of artisanal products, including textiles, ceramics, and traditional Colombian accessories. It's a convenient destination for those looking to combine upscale shopping with authentic souvenirs.

Highlights:

- Handwoven Accessories: Find beautifully crafted scarves, hats, and bags made from locally sourced materials, showcasing Colombia's textile expertise.
- Ceramic Art: Explore stalls featuring hand-painted ceramics and pottery, often adorned with intricate patterns inspired by indigenous designs.
- Traditional Colombian Masks: Take home a unique piece of Colombian culture with traditional masks crafted by skilled artisans, each with its own symbolic significance.

Plaza de Usaquén Artisan Market

Location: Usaquén neighborhood, Bogotá

- Usaquén, known for its charming ambiance, hosts an artisan market in its picturesque main square. The market showcases the work of local artists and craftsmen, offering a range of handmade goods, from woven textiles to indigenous-inspired art. The cobblestone streets and historic surroundings add to the allure of this market, making it a delightful place to find unique souvenirs.

Highlights:

- Indigenous-inspired Art: Browse through stalls featuring paintings, sculptures, and crafts inspired by Colombia's indigenous cultures, each piece telling a unique story.
- Handcrafted Toys: Discover traditional Colombian toys and games, perfect for a nostalgic and culturally rich souvenir.
- Artisanal Home Decor: Usaquén's market offers an array of artisanal home decor items, from hand-painted tiles to intricately carved wooden pieces.

General Tips for Souvenir Shopping in Bogotá:

- Bargaining: In open-air markets and certain shops, bargaining is common. It's a cultural practice, so don't hesitate to negotiate the price, but do so respectfully.
- Authenticity: If authenticity is important to you, seek out items made by local artisans. Look for artisan markets and cooperative shops that directly support the creators.
- Ask About Origins: Engage with vendors and ask about the origins and stories behind the items. Many souvenirs carry cultural significance, and learning about them enhances their value.
- Packaging and Fragility: Consider the fragility of the items you're purchasing, especially if they are delicate or easily breakable. Ensure that vendors provide suitable packaging for safe transport.

Bogotá's souvenirs offer a piece of Colombian culture and craftsmanship that you can carry home with you. Whether you choose traditional textiles, indigenous-inspired art, or vintage treasures, each item becomes a tangible memory of your journey through the vibrant streets of Bogotá.*

Chapter 12

Practical Travel Tips

Safety and Security Tips for Travelers in Bogotá

Bogotá, like any major city, has its unique characteristics and considerations when it comes to safety. While the city has made significant strides in improving security, it's essential for travelers to stay informed and take precautions to ensure a safe and enjoyable visit. Here are comprehensive safety and security tips for travelers exploring Bogotá:

1. Stay Informed:

Local Customs and Laws:

- Research: Familiarize yourself with local customs, laws, and cultural norms before arriving. Understanding the cultural context enhances your overall safety.

Travel Advisories:

- Check Advisories: Stay updated on travel advisories from your government's travel department. Be aware of any potential risks or warnings for the region.

2. Transportation Safety:

Use Authorized Transportation:

- Taxis: Use authorized taxi services or reputable ride-hailing apps. Confirm that the taxi has a visible ID and operates with a meter.

Public Transportation:

- TransMilenio and SITP: Keep an eye on your belongings in crowded public transportation. Use secure bags and pockets to prevent pickpocketing.

3. Personal Belongings:

Secure Valuables:

- Avoid Flashy Items: Keep expensive jewelry, electronics, and valuables discreet to avoid attracting unnecessary attention.

Anti-Theft Bags:

- Use Secure Bags: Consider using anti-theft bags with features like lockable zippers and RFID blocking.

4. Money Matters:

ATM Safety:

- Use ATMs in Safe Areas: Withdraw cash from ATMs in well-lit, busy areas, and be cautious of your surroundings.

Emergency Cash:

- Have Backup Funds: Carry a small amount of emergency cash in a separate location.

5. Accommodation Safety:

Choose Reputable Accommodations:

- Read Reviews: Research and choose reputable accommodations with positive reviews for safety and security.

Room Safety:

- Secure Your Room: Use hotel safes for valuables and secure doors and windows properly.

6. Health and Well-being:

Health Precautions:

- Vaccinations: Ensure that routine vaccinations are up-to-date, and check if any specific vaccinations are recommended for your trip.

Emergency Contacts:

- Know Local Emergency Numbers: Familiarize yourself with local emergency numbers, including the contact information for your embassy or consulate.

7. Navigating Neighborhoods:

Be Informed:

- Research Neighborhoods: Understand the characteristics of different neighborhoods. While many areas are safe, it's essential to be aware of your surroundings.

Local Advice:

- Ask Locals: Seek advice from locals or your accommodation about safe routes and areas to explore.

8. Language Skills:

Learn Basic Phrases:

- Spanish Phrases: While many people in Bogotá speak English, learning some basic Spanish phrases can be helpful and enhance your overall safety.

9. Emergency Preparedness:

Emergency Kit:

- Carry Essentials: Have a small emergency kit with basic first aid supplies, a flashlight, and important medications.

Know Evacuation Routes:

- Hotel Information: Know the emergency evacuation routes and procedures at your accommodation.

10. Cultural Sensitivity:

Respect Local Customs:

- Cultural Sensitivity: Show respect for local customs and traditions to foster positive interactions with locals.

Dress Modestly:

- Appropriate Attire: In more conservative areas, dress modestly to avoid unwanted attention.

Bogotá is a city with a rich cultural tapestry and warm hospitality, but like any destination, it requires travelers to exercise caution and stay informed. By following these safety and security tips, you can enhance your overall experience in Bogotá and ensure a memorable and secure visit to this dynamic capital.

Essential Packing Checklists

Packing for your trip to Bogotá requires a thoughtful selection of items to ensure you're prepared for the city's diverse experiences, varying weather, and unique cultural activities. Use this comprehensive checklist to make sure you have everything you need for a comfortable and enjoyable stay in Colombia's vibrant capital.

Travel Essentials:

Passport and Travel Documents:

- Ensure your passport is valid for at least six months.
- Print or have digital copies of travel confirmations, hotel reservations, and important contact information.

Travel Insurance:

- Carry a copy of your travel insurance policy and emergency contact information.

Money and Banking:

- Notify your bank about your travel dates.
- Bring local currency (Colombian Pesos) for small purchases and transportation.

Prescription Medications:

- Pack enough prescription medications for the duration of your stay.
- Carry a copy of your prescriptions.

Basic First Aid Kit:

- Include band-aids, pain relievers, antidiarrheal medication, and any personal medical items.

Clothing and Accessories:

Weather-Appropriate Clothing:

- Lightweight clothing for warmer days and layers for cooler evenings.
- A waterproof jacket or poncho for occasional rain.

Comfortable Shoes:

- Walking shoes for exploring the city and potentially uneven terrain.

Adapters and Chargers:

- Power adapters for Colombian outlets.
- Chargers for your electronic devices.

Daypack or Small Backpack:

- For daily excursions, carrying water, snacks, and essentials.

Personal Items:

Toiletries:

- Toothbrush, toothpaste, and other personal hygiene items.
- Sunscreen and insect repellent.

Travel-Sized Laundry Detergent:

- In case you need to do laundry during your stay.

Travel Towel:

- Quick-drying and compact for convenience.

Electronics and Gadgets:

Camera and Accessories:

- Capture the moments with your camera and don't forget extra memory cards.

Portable Charger:

- Keep your devices charged on the go.

Cultural and Practical Items:

Spanish Phrasebook:

- While many locals speak English, having some basic phrases can enhance your experience.

Reusable Water Bottle:

- Stay hydrated, especially at higher altitudes.

Travel Umbrella:

- A compact umbrella for unexpected rain showers.

Optional Items:

Guidebook:

- A guidebook for Bogotá and Colombia can be a helpful resource.

Travel Journal:

- Document your experiences and memories.

Snacks:

- Pack some non-perishable snacks for energy during day trips.

For Outdoor Activities:

Hiking Gear:

- If planning on hiking, bring suitable footwear and clothing.

Daypack:

- For longer hikes or outdoor adventures.

Important Notes:

Altitude Considerations:

- Bogotá is at a high altitude, so be aware of potential altitude-related symptoms. Bring any prescribed medications if you have altitude sickness concerns.

Security Precautions:

- Use a money belt or secure pouch for valuables, especially in crowded areas.

Local Customs:

- Respectful attire is appreciated when visiting religious sites.

COVID-19 Considerations:

- Follow current travel advisories and health guidelines.
- Carry hand sanitizer and a mask for crowded places.

Adapt this checklist based on your personal preferences, the duration of your stay, and planned activities. Bogotá's dynamic atmosphere awaits, and being well-prepared ensures you can fully enjoy the city's cultural richness and diverse offerings.

Chapter 13

Conclusion

Fond Farewell: Reflecting on Your Bogotá Adventure

As your Bogotá adventure comes to an end, take a moment to reflect on the rich experiences and vibrant moments that defined your journey through Colombia's capital. Bogotá, with its unique blend of history, culture, and modernity, has likely left an indelible mark on your travel memories. Here's a contemplative look at bidding farewell to Bogotá:

Reflecting on Your Time in Bogotá:

Cultural Immersion: Consider the cultural immersion you experienced, from exploring historic neighborhoods like La Candelaria to engaging with local artisans in bustling markets.

Culinary Delights: Reflect on the diverse flavors you sampled, from traditional Colombian dishes to street food delights. Recall the aroma of coffee wafting through markets and the taste of local specialties.

Architectural Marvels: Contemplate the awe-inspiring architecture that dots the cityscape, from colonial-era gems to contemporary structures that reflect Bogotá's evolving identity.

Local Connections: Cherish the connections made with locals, whether through shared conversations, the vibrant arts scene, or the warm hospitality encountered throughout your journey.

Capturing Memories:

Photographic Mementos: Your camera or smartphone gallery is likely filled with snapshots of Bogotá's landscapes, vibrant street art, and the smiling faces of locals. Take time to curate these visual memories.

Journal Entries: If you kept a travel journal, revisit your entries to relive the details of each day, the emotions stirred by new experiences, and the personal growth gained from your Bogotá adventure.

Expressing Gratitude:

Thankful Moments: Consider the aspects of your trip that brought gratitude—whether it's the helpful guidance of a local, the unexpected kindness of a fellow traveler, or the sheer beauty of the landscapes.

Appreciation for Diversity: Acknowledge the diversity encountered in Bogotá, both in its people and its landscapes. Reflect on how this diversity enriched your travel experience.

Beyond Bogotá: Exploring More of Colombia

While saying goodbye to Bogotá may bring a tinge of melancholy, Colombia has much more to offer for those with an adventurous spirit. Consider extending your exploration beyond the capital to uncover the diverse wonders that await in other regions of this captivating country:

1. Cartagena and the Caribbean Coast:

Colonial Charm: Explore the enchanting streets of Cartagena, a UNESCO World Heritage site, with its well-preserved colonial architecture and vibrant street life.

Caribbean Delights: Relax on the Caribbean coast's white-sand beaches, snorkel in crystal-clear waters, and savor the region's unique culinary offerings.

2. Medellín and the Coffee Region:

Innovative Medellín: Discover the innovative spirit of Medellín, a city known for its urban transformation, modern art scene, and botanical gardens.

Coffee Country: Immerse yourself in the lush landscapes of the Coffee Triangle, where you can tour coffee plantations, hike through scenic valleys, and experience Colombian coffee culture.

3. Amazon Rainforest and Leticia:

Amazon Adventure: Embark on an Amazon Rainforest adventure from the town of Leticia, exploring dense jungles, encountering diverse wildlife, and navigating the Amazon River.

Indigenous Culture: Learn about the rich indigenous cultures that call the Amazon home, gaining insights into their traditions and way of life.

4. Tayrona National Natural Park:

Coastal Wilderness: Head to Tayrona National Natural Park for a taste of untouched coastal wilderness, with hiking trails leading to pristine beaches, ancient ruins, and dense jungles.

5. Villa de Leyva and Boyacá:

Colonial Gem: Visit the charming town of Villa de Leyva, known for its cobblestone streets, whitewashed buildings, and the expansive Plaza Mayor.

Boyacá's Heritage: Explore the cultural and historical heritage of Boyacá, with its picturesque landscapes, traditional festivals, and indigenous traditions.

Planning Your Next Colombian Adventure:

Research and Inspiration: Dive into research about your next destination, seeking inspiration from travel guides, local recommendations, and fellow travelers.

Local Experiences: Plan to engage in local experiences that resonate with the unique character of each region, whether it's immersing yourself in indigenous cultures, enjoying outdoor adventures, or savoring regional cuisines.

As you bid farewell to Bogotá and open the door to further explorations in Colombia, remember that your journey is a collection of moments—each one contributing to the rich tapestry of your travel story. Cherish the memories, express gratitude for the experiences, and embrace the anticipation of new adventures that await in this diverse and captivating country. Bogotá may be the beginning, but Colombia has so much more to unveil on your travel odyssey. Safe travels and may your Colombian adventures continue to unfold with wonder and discovery.

Made in the USA
Monee, IL
27 September 2024